New Studies in the Philosophy of Religion

General Editor: W. D. Hudson, Reader in Moral Philosoohy,
University of Exeter

This series of monographs includes studies of all the main
problems in the philosophy of religion. It will be of particular
interest to those who study this subject in universities or colleges.
The philosophical problems connected with religious belief are
not, however, a subject of concern only to specialists; they arise
in one form or another for all intelligent men when confronted
by the appeals or the claims of religion.

The general approach of this series is from the standpoint of
contemporary analytical philosophy, and the monographs are
written by a distinguished team of philosophers, all of whom
now teach, or have recently taught, in British or American
universities. Each author has been commissioned to analyse
some aspect of religious belief; to set forth clearly and concisely
the philosophical problems which arise from it; to take into
account the solutions which classical or contemporary philosophers have offered; and to present his own critical assessment
of how religious belief now stands in the light of these problems
and their proposed solutions.

In the main it is theism with which these monographs deal,
because that is the type of religious belief with which readers
are most likely to be familiar, but other forms of religion are not
ignored. Some of the authors are religious believers and some
are not, but it is not their primary aim to write polemically,
much less dogmatically, for or against religion. Rather, they
set themselves to clarify the nature of religious belief in the light
of modern philosophy by bringing into focus the questions about
it which a reasonable man as such has to ask. How is talk of
God like, and how unlike, other universes of discourse in which
men engage, such as science, art or morality? Is this talk of
God self-consistent? Does it accord with other rational beliefs
which we hold about man or the world which he inhabits? It
is questions such as these which this series will help the reader
to answer for himself.

New Studies in the Philosophy of Religion

IN THE SAME SERIES

Published

In preparation

The Logical Status of 'God'

and

The Function of Theological Sentences

MICHAEL DURRANT

Senior Lecturer in Philosophy, University College, Cardiff

Macmillan
St. Martin's Press

First published 1973 by
THE MACMILLAN PRESS LTD
London and Basingstoke
Associated companies in New York Toronto
Dublin Melbourne Johannesburg and Madras

Library of Congress catalog card no. 73–93886

SBN 333 13347 1

Printed in Great Britain by
R & R CLARK LTD
Edinburgh

Contents

General Editor's Preface

In contemporary philosophy of religion the central issue is undoubtedly whether or not it makes sense to speak in terms of God. This is the issue with which Mr Durrant's monograph is concerned. Since the dawn of philosophy, men have always argued as to whether or not religious beliefs are true; but in recent times it has been recognised that there is an even more fundamental problem, namely whether or not religious beliefs can be meaningful. If they cannot, then of course the question of their truth or falsity does not arise.

Mr Durrant, in this book, reviews with admirable clarity, the work which philosophers have been doing in recent years on this central issue and adds his own valuable contribution to the discussion. He is alive to the extreme complexity of God-talk and his approach is the reverse of dogmatic or question-begging. University teachers and students, working in the philosophy of religion will find this monograph most useful as an introduction to the logical problems involved in religious language; but a wider readership, consisting of all those who wish to make up their minds about religion in the light of the most recent philosophical reflection on this vital subject, will, I think, find a careful study of this book most rewarding.

University of Exeter   W. D. HUDSON

Preface

My concern in this essay is with the logical status of 'God' in the sense of an item of religious language with a view to determining the function or possible functions of sentences of the form 'God is F', where 'F', from the standpoint of grammar is an adjective or adjectival expression which is such that the predicable '—— is F' (in Professor Geach's sense as introduced in *Reference and Generality*, chapter 2) is able to yield true or false predications of individual human beings as subjects. Examples of sentences of such a form will be: 'God is loving'; 'God is wise'; 'God is good'. In order to cater for some features of religious language, it will also be necessary to consider sentences of the form 'God is infinitely F', for in some cases God is 'spoken of' not only in terms of being F but of being infinitely F (infinitely loving, infinitely wise, infinitely good, etc.).

I shall first make the assumption that sentences of the form 'God is F' can be used and indeed are used to express true propositions and hence I shall be concerned to investigate what the form of such propositions so expressed might be. The possible form of such propositions, however, crucially depends upon the logical status of 'God' as an item of religious language, i.e. the role or roles which the sign "God" has in that language. It depends upon whether 'God' as an item of that language is a proper name, an abbreviated definite description either of the form 'The God of A' (where 'A' is a proper name) or 'The one and only F', a descriptive predicable term (Frege's *Begriffswort*), a special kind of descriptive predicable term (general term) such as Professor Geach's 'substantival general term' or an abstract term.

In my first chapter I shall argue for the thesis that 'God' is not a proper name and hence that on one count sentences of the form I have introduced cannot be regarded as expressing propositions of a subject–predicate type, since whilst it is not a necessary condition of 'A' being able to occur as the logical subject of a proposition that 'A' should be a proper name, it is a sufficient condition of 'A' being so able to occur. In my second chapter I shall raise the question as to whether 'God', if not a proper name, can nevertheless stand as a logical subject, i.e. whether 'God' as either a definite description of a certain form or a substantival general term in Geach's sense can so stand. This will involve a discussion of whether (a) definite descriptions of a certain form can (in general) so stand and (b) whether general terms of a substantival type can so stand. My third chapter raises a number of potential difficulties for the thesis much advocated by Professor Geach, namely that 'God' is a descriptive predicable term (Frege's *Begriffswort*). I maintain that, in some types of occurrence at least, 'God' is not such, but on the contrary is an abstract term. In the light of this latter consideration I raise the question as to what form of proposition sentences of the form 'God is F' can be said to express, where 'God' is an abstract term. Having rejected Strawson's thesis that 'anything whatever' can stand as a logical subject and that abstract terms can so stand, I consider various alternatives for the form of proposition which sentences of the above form might be said to express, all of which I contend fail for differing and interesting reasons. In Chapter Four I explicitly reject the assumption that sentences of the form I have been considering are to be taken as expressing propositions and consider some alternative accounts, viz. that they are to be taken as expressing 'grammatical remarks' in Wittgenstein's sense and that they are to be regarded as presenting 'pictures'. I consider two recent attempts to develop this latter view. Both types of account, I shall argue, break down in various ways for different reasons.

It is my conclusion that it is not possible to offer a coherent account of the logical status of 'God' as an item of Christian language as a whole, since 'God' exhibits differing and indeed incompatible statūs. Neither is it possible to offer a tenable account of the function of sentences of the form I am considering even if one rejects the contention that such sentences have a proposition-expressing role. Indeed, I argue for the thesis that such sentences must have a proposition-expressing role in at least *some* types of case for their role in other types of case to be intelligible. However, I am led to conclude that any attempt to set out a scheme in which 'God' has a single logical status such that a coherent and consistent account of the form of proposition expressed by sentences of the above form can be offered, is doomed to failure. No such scheme can cope with the manifold and inconsistent logic of 'God'.

The problems and difficulties raised in this essay are problems and difficulties which readily beset anyone who becomes interested in religious language via an interest in problems in Philosophical Logic at an elementary level, but this essay has not been written solely with such persons in mind. Such problems and difficulties need to be brought to the attention of others for they are not problems and difficulties which any serious-minded person honestly concerned with religious belief can afford to ignore. There are those who will say: 'But one should not be concerned with religious language but with the reality which lies behind it'. However religious language is not contingently related to the reality which it expresses and in order to speak sensibly of 'the reality which lies behind it', we must be able to express such reality. As Professor Geach has rightly commented: 'A man may *assert* that God is too high a subject matter for human argument: but having said this he had best keep silence, for if he *argues* the matter he at once contradicts himself' (*God and the Soul*, p. 105).

I am indebted to Mrs M. Rees for typing the manuscript of this essay and to my wife for her persistent encouragement and patience whilst I have been grappling with these problems.

Cardiff
March 1972

Michael Durrant

Some Notes on Technical Terms Introduced in this Essay

Begriffswort	Cf. Frege, in P. T. Geach and M. Black, *Philosophical Writings of Gottlob Frege* (Basil Blackwell, Oxford, 1952), pp. 45, 48; *Foundations of Arithmetic*, trans. J. L. Austin (Basil Blackwell, Oxford, 1950), pp. 63–6.
Concept (cf. Chapter 3)	Used in Frege's sense (ibid.).
General term	An expression which can apply to or be satisfied by many individuals.
Logical subject	What can occur as a logical subject is a type of expression. The type of expression that can so occur is that type which is such that it can be used to identifyingly refer to, i.e. to pick out an individual (cf. Strawson, *Individuals*, chapter I, sections [1] and [2]). That type of expression is said to introduce a subject of predication (which is an entity, not an expression) when it occurs in the context of a whole sentence which purports to tell us something about that which is so identifyingly referred to.
Predicable	Used in Professor Geach's sense (*Reference and Generality*, p. 25).
Predicate	An expression that gives us a proposition about something if we attach it to another expression that identifyingly refers to some-

thing which we are making the proposition about.

Proposition That which is either true or false, but which may or may not be asserted. Sentences are said to *express* propositions but they cannot be identified with them since (i) sentences themselves are not either true or false; (ii) different sentences may express the same proposition (e.g. 'John is taller than Jack' and 'Jack is shorter than John' express the same proposition, where 'John' and 'Jack' have the same reference in each case); (iii) the same sentence may express different propositions (e.g. 'John Snooks is bald' expresses a different proposition on occasions of utterance (a) and (b) if, on occasions of utterance (a) and (b), 'John Snooks' has different references).

Term In its use in this essay, 'term' signifies a linguistic item; a term is an expression, not an entity.

1 On Whether 'God' is a Proper Name

I shall first investigate whether 'God' is a proper name, for if the answer to this question is in the affirmative then sentences of the form 'God is F' can be said to express propositions of a subject–predicate type, for whilst it is not a necessary condition of an expression being able to occur as a logical subject, introducing a subject of predication, that such an expression is a proper name, it is a sufficient condition.

1. It may be thought that 'God' is a proper name in Christian writing from, for example, the opening phrases of the following prayers:

 (i) O God, from whom all holy desires, all good counsels and all just works do proceed. . . .

 (ii) O God, we have heard with our ears and our fathers have declared unto us, the noble works thou didst in their days and in the old time before them. . . .

 (iii) O God, whose nature and property is ever to have mercy and to forgive, receive our humble petitions. . . .[1]

but such examples do not show this for it is not a sufficient condition of an expression being a proper name that the personal pronoun and personal relative pronoun can be used in connection with it. Such personal pronouns can be used in connection with descriptions, yet descriptions are not a type of name at all, let alone proper names. Indeed, as I shall argue, we must radically and clearly distinguish between names and descriptions. As examples of such personal pronouns going with descriptions we might have:

O man, who has brought thyself to utter degradation. . . .

or

Man, thou hast gone astray following thine own whims and desires. . . .

1

or, again, we might have:

> O thou one and only God from whom all holy desires, all
> good counsels, and all just works do proceed. . . .
> O thou one and only God who has prepared for them that
> love thee such good things as pass man's understanding. . . .

That indeed 'God' is not a proper name in the context of
these prayers can be shown by the fact that in other prayers in
which the vocative could equally well be substituted, 'God' is a
description, a general term. In these cases 'God' is prefaced by
such items as 'almighty', 'everlasting' and 'merciful'. For
example:

> (iv) Almighty God, the fountain of all goodness, we humbly
> beseech thee to bless *Elizabeth* the Queen Mother . . .
>
> (v) Almighty and Everlasting God, who alone workest
> great marvels . . .
>
> (vi) Almighty and merciful God, of whose only gift it cometh
> that thy faithful people do unto thee true and laudable
> service. . . .[2]

However it is impossible that proper names should be so prefaced. Where a proper name is, in fact, so prefaced this is merely
a convenient way of speaking about the attributes which purportedly hold true of the bearer of the name as an entity of such
and such a kind indicated by a general term. For example, if
we were to introduce the phrase 'almighty and everlasting
Socrates' this would be to speak of the almighty and everlasting
man Socrates, granted that 'Socrates' here had the use of the
proper name of the philosopher who lived in fifth-century
Athens. One cannot say here: 'But the individual Socrates can
be almighty and everlasting in his own right without being an
almighty *such and such*, such that "almighty" and "everlasting"
go with the name'. 'Almighty' and 'everlasting' logically must
go with the general term which provides the replacement for
'such and such' since (a) for Socrates to exist *is* for Socrates to
be a *such and such* – as Aristotle pointed out in the *Posterior
Analytics* (92b 14ff.), there is no such class as the class of things
which simply *are*; and (b) 'almighty' and 'everlasting' are
attributive adjectival terms[3] and hence do require a completion
in the form of a general term. We have to understand what is
involved in the use of the general term in order to understand

2

what it is to say that something falling under that term is almighty or everlasting.

Further, there are other prayers in which the vocative 'O God' in the original examples is replaced by or could be replaced by general terms or descriptions where such general terms or descriptions are its equivalent.

For example:

(vii) Grant, O Lord, we beseech thee that the course of this world may be so peaceably ordered. . . .

(viii) Lord of all power and might who art the author and giver of all good things. . . .

(ix) Grant to us, Lord, we beseech thee, the spirit to think and do such things as be rightful. . . .[4]

Yet no one can claim that either 'Lord' or 'Lord of all power and might' are proper names; they are clearly descriptions which may apply to one or more objects in a given sense or use. A proper name can only name one object in a given use of that name. 'Lord' can sensibly be prefaced by 'one', 'many', or 'several'; as the scripture says: 'There are Lords many and Gods many', but proper names cannot be so prefaced. Cases in which they are apparently so prefaced are simply elliptical ways of speaking. If one were to assert that there are many Aristotles or many Johns, this would simply be an elliptical way of saying that there are many (e.g.) men who are called by those names. The prefaces 'one', 'many' and 'several' logically go with the general terms which can replace the blank in the formulation: 'There (is) are one, many, several ——'s which bear the name "Aristotle" or "John"'. That this is so follows from the truth that for 'A' to be a proper name is for 'A' to be the proper name of a *such and such* (to coin Professor Anscombe's formulation[5]), where 'such and such' is a general term of a certain kind, i.e. one which can at least furnish us with what Professor Geach calls 'a criterion of continued identity'[6]. It would only be possible to take 'there are many Aristotles and many Johns' in a non-elliptical way if (a) one radically confused proper names and descriptions (general terms) thus giving proper names the status of descriptions or (b) maintained the impossible thesis that in order for 'A' to be a proper name it is not necessary that 'A' be the proper name of some object falling under a description of a certain kind. That this thesis is impossible has been

3

well put by Miss Anscombe.[7] It is impossible since on this thesis it is not *possible* to specify the bearer of the name or to decide that the name has the same reference on two or more occasions of use.

Thus far I have been concerned to illustrate and argue that from actual occurrences of 'God' in religious language, 'God' does not have the status of a proper name, in spite of some initial appearances to the contrary. Rather, from the cases so far examined, it seems that it is either a general term like 'man' or more specifically a definite description such that for any occurrence of 'God' we can substitute 'The one and only God'. At this point the following comment may be made: 'Why cannot we say that in some contexts 'God' is a proper name (as at least initially suggested by (i)–(iii) above), whereas in other contexts (such as (iv)–(vi) above), 'God' is a description?' To so say however would be indirectly to accuse Christianity of employing its central word in radically incompatible ways, for no word can genuinely be both a proper name and a description (general term). It will not do, at this stage, to go for a 'multiplicity of uses' thesis when two of these uses are radically incompatible – unless one wishes to start off by levelling the charge of incompatible uses. That we must make a clear and radical distinction between names and general terms or descriptions is apparent since a name stands for or has stood for an object or names some object whereas, on the contrary, a description does not stand for or name anything. Rather, a description is satisfied by something or other and we must clearly distinguish the relation of standing for or naming from that of satisfaction, as Russell did in his Theory of Descriptions. As Professor Anscombe has said commenting on Russell's theory:

> At first sight, one readily assumes that, if the sentences in which descriptions occur are true, each description stands for an object and the rest of the sentence expresses what holds of the object. To say this is to compare descriptions with (real) proper names; but at the same time the way in which descriptions stand for objects must be different from the way in which proper names stand for objects; indeed, the consideration of this leads to a breakdown of the idea that descriptions 'stand for' at all.

4

This is most obvious for indefinite descriptions, but it is also true of definite descriptions. A proper name will stand for its object because that object is called by that name; but a description, if it stands for its object, does so because the object satisfies it, which is clearly quite a different relation.[8]

That it is of crucial importance to distinguish between names and descriptions has also been well argued by Geach in *Reference and Generality*.[9] He there argues that:

> . . . names and predicables are absolutely different. A name has a complete sense and can stand by itself in a simple act of naming[10]; a predicable, on the other hand, is a potential predicate, and a predicate never has a complete sense, since it does not show what the predication is about: it is what is left of a proposition when the subject is removed and thus essentially contains an empty place to be filled by a subject. And though a predicable may occur in a proposition otherwise than as a predicate attached to a subject, it does not then lose its predicative, incomplete character; it has sense only as contributing towards the sense of a proposition, not at all by itself.
>
> A predicable applies to or is true of things. . . . This relation must be sharply distinguished from the relation of name to bearer. . . .
>
> A predicable never names what it is true of. . . .

Further, Geach points out, predicables always occur in contradictory pairs and by attaching such a pair to a common subject we get a contradictory pair of propositions. On the contrary, we never have a pair of names so related that by attaching the same predicates to both we always get a pair of contradictory propositions. Finally, tenses attach to predicables as well as to propositions but names, as Aristotle observed, are tenseless.

Someone might comment here that it is not clear that one can equate what I have previously termed 'descriptions' (following Russell) with Geach's 'predicables'. I do not think there is any inherent objection to such an equation, for Russell points out that a description is an incomplete symbol. It only has sense as contributing towards the sense of a proposition and is precisely to be distinguished from a complete symbol (a 'simple' symbol) which has independent sense in that it names an object. The possible difficulties which arise for any equation

5

of Russell's descriptions with Geach's predicables arise over Russell's contention that descriptions are complex symbols: their meaning is a function of certain more elementary symbols and ultimately a function of 'simple' symbols, which include not only the proper names of 'individuals' (in Russell's special sense of 'individual') but signs for 'universals'. Geach's theory of predicables does not commit him, as far as I can judge, to any such theory. It is not, however, misleading to say that for Russell, as for Geach, a description (a predicable) essentially has the form '—— is F', whether the description be indefinite or definite, such that 'man' has the form '—— is a man' and 'the present King of France' has the form: '—— is the present King of France'. This is not to say that Russell analyses propositions containing such indefinite or definite descriptions into propositions of such a form. He clearly does not. Any proposition containing an indefinite description such as 'a man' is analysed out as:

'C (x) and x is human' is not always false.[11]

A proposition containing a definite description, say, 'the father of Charles II' as in 'The father of Charles II was executed' is analysed out as:

It is not always false of x that x begat Charles II and that x was executed and that 'if y begat Charles II, y is identical with x' is always true of y.

But it is one thing to say what the essential form of a description is and another to offer an analysis of propositions containing such a description.

It might be further objected that definite descriptions must be radically distinguished from indefinite descriptions on the grounds that whilst indefinite descriptions can apply to or be satisfied by any number of objects definite descriptions can only be satisfied by or apply to any one object. But this consideration is not a sufficient basis for a radical distinction; it would only be a sufficient basis for a radical distinction if for 'can only be satisfied by any one object', we have to write 'can only be satisfied by one object', which is not the case. A parallel objection to the effect that a definite description cannot be regarded as a predicable in Geach's sense, since a predicable applies to or is true of things, likewise breaks down, for whilst a definite description only applies to any one object, this does not imply

6

that it can apply to only one object. The consideration that a
definite description can only apply to any one object does not
thereby rule out our talking in terms of 'applying' or 'being
true of'.

A further objection may be pressed at this point, namely, that
definite descriptions are not potential predicates (and hence not
predicables) since they do not have the role of telling us anything about an object, but, on the contrary, have that of
identifying an object. I do not deny that definite descriptions
may have the role of identifying objects for us when they occur
in the grammatically predicative position, but this does not
deter from their essentially predicative status, since a condition
of their performing such a role is that they are already satisfied
by or hold true of the individual named by the subject expression. I therefore do not see any inherent objection to saying
that descriptions, either indefinite or definite, essentially have
the form '—— is F'. Whereas, on the contrary, 'Socrates' and
'Aristotle' distinctly do not have this form and cannot be construed as '—— is Socrates' and '—— is Aristotle'.[12]

It may be counteracted, by those who are adherents of
Professor Strawson's account of the way in which definite
descriptions have meaning, that definite descriptions have
meaning in that whilst it is not necessary that they do refer on
every occasion of use, there are some occasions of use on which
they do refer and that they have meaning in that they can be
so used. Such definite descriptions do not have sense in that
they contribute to the sense of a proposition. I shall, however,
be discussing Strawson's claim in my next chapter and offering
reasons for rejecting it. *Here* my point is solely that we must
carefully and radically distinguish between names and descriptions.

My case thus far then is that, in spite of some appearances to
the contrary, 'God', from the examples earlier considered, is a
descriptive term in Christian language and not a proper name
and I have attempted to explain why it cannot be both.

2. That some philosophers and theologians *have* thought 'God'
to be a proper name can be seen as follows:

A.

Because the primary subject of theological statements is,

7

according to unbelievers, preposterous and, according to believers, 'transcendent', the statements about Him cannot be anything but parables borrowed from the world of our more direct acquaintance. And since He is by supposition very different from those things or persons . . . (Austin Farrer, 'Examination of Theological Belief')[13]

The context here makes it clear that Dr Farrer regards 'God' as the proper name of a transcendent being (cf. also the top of p. 11, where 'God' is replaced by the personal pronoun 'He'; p. 12, 'In one sense the parables are applied to God and His action. But in another sense the whole parabolic discourse about God and His action is applied to life'; p. 30 (last paragraph), 'For the personal claim which meets him on every hand is exerted not simply by men, but by God. So the Christian may think but he must not suppose that such a fact about God can conceivably stand alone').

B. Commenting on St Paul's *Epistle to the Corinthians*, C.2, vv. 9–15, Dr Farrer says: 'It will be seen that St Paul works from the analogy between divine self-disclosure and human self-disclosure' and then adds:

But he is unable to make a straightforward development of it. For whereas our friends disclose their thoughts to us by speech, none of us claims to have heard the tongue of God or even supposes that he has a tongue (Austin Farrer, 'Revelation').[14]

It would be very difficult to deny that here Dr Farrer conceives of 'God' as the proper name of a transcendent entity and indeed this construction is consistent with the passages cited from the earlier article and with his later comment:

'Revelation' means 'personal self disclosure' but that the analogy from our friends' utterances will not bear a plain application to God.[15]

It must, however, be pointed out that in some contexts Dr Farrer *does* regard 'God' as a description, as witness the following:

(i) The God about whom and to whom believers speak is the self revealing God: the 'God of pure reason' is scarcely encountered outside philosophical argument.[16]

(ii) . . . And, as we said in the body of our argument, the God who makes claims upon us through our fellows is taken to be their maker and redeemer.[17]

I thus conclude that Dr Farrer does make the impossible demand that 'God' is both a proper name and a description. Unfortunately he is not the only writer to make such a demand.

C.

Thus when we say that God and Mr Jones are both good or that they are both beings, remembering that the content which the word 'good' or 'being' has for us is derived from our experience of goodness . . . we are so far as the analogy of attribution is concerned, saying no more than that God has goodness or being in whatever way is necessary, if he is able to produce goodness and being in his creatures (E. L. Mascall, *Existence and Analogy*, p. 102).

It is clear that here at least Professor Mascall is treating 'God' as an ordinary proper name like 'Jones' to which he directly relates it.

D.

The religious man is aware of a certain peculiar type of resistance being set up within the sphere of his values: the resistance, namely, of absolute, sacred, unconditional values . . . it is in and through the accent of unconditionality that the awareness of meeting another's will in and through such values is given. . . . Whose will is it, then, that is met in such unconditional value resistance? To the religious mind it is the will of God. And 'will' means 'person' (H. H. Farmer, *The World and God*, p. 23 ff.).

On Farmer's account 'God' is the proper name of a 'will' or 'person', which 'will' the religious man is said to come up against in 'Divine Encounter'.[18]

E.

We are holding that our knowledge of God rests rather on the revelation of His Personal Presence as Father, Son, and Holy Spirit . . . Of such a Presence it must be true that to those who have never been confronted with it argument is

9

useless, whilst to those who have it is superfluous (John Baillie, *Our Knowledge of God*, p. 132).

On Baillie's account, 'God' is the proper name of a 'personal presence' exhibited in the persons of the Holy Trinity.

Many more examples of 'God' occurring as a proper name in the writings of theologians and philosophers can be cited, but I shall not cite them here.[19] Indeed it does not seem extravagant to say that most, if not all, 'Encounter Theologies' do treat 'God' as a proper name – more particularly as the proper name of a person or a personal presence or a variant on these (e.g. Farmer's 'will').

3. Granted that some philosophers and theologians have indeed treated 'God' as a proper name, what difficulties are there in accepting this view?

First it is necessary to turn to a writer who maintains that whilst 'God' is in some sense a proper name, it does not meet the requirements for an expression being a proper name in a fully fledged sense and hence it is an 'improper proper name'. This writer is Mr I. M. Crombie in his influential paper 'The Possibility of Theological Statements'.[20] A perusal of some of the points Crombie raises will help us see some of the difficulties in maintaining the view that 'God' is a proper name.

Crombie claims that one can sensibly raise the question 'Who is God?' – that this is a proper question to ask parallel to asking 'Who is Tom?' if it is asserted that Tom loves Mary. It is on the basis of the askability of this question that 'God' can be said, initially at any rate, to be a proper name, even though 'God' does not meet the second of his requirements for any expression being a proper name. Now, whilst it is true that if 'A' is a proper name one can indeed ask, and it is necessary to ask, of whom or what 'A' is the proper name, it can be argued (initially at any rate) that if 'A' occurs as the putative subject in sentences expressing a proposition of a subject–predicate kind or if 'A' occurs as a putative name in a sentence expressing a relational proposition, it does not follow that (a) 'A' is a proper name or that (b) one can ask the question 'Who or what is A?' For it is at least initially plausible to argue (i) that some general terms can occur as logical subjects (Geach's 'substantivals')[21] or as names in a relational proposition, and

10

(ii) that some definite descriptions can occur in such roles. Yet one cannot ask of such general terms or such definite descriptions as so occurring 'Who or what is A?' in Crombie's sense of that question, for Crombie's sense of that question seeks an answer in terms of a definite description which will enable us to identify an individual. Crombie's case for saying that one *can* ask 'Who is God?' depends at least upon the contention that any expression which can occur as a logical subject is a proper name, or at least has a *prima facie* case for being said to be a proper name. Yet neither Geach's 'substantivals' nor definite descriptions of the form 'The so and so' are proper names or even names, even though Geach does claim that the former can have the use of names. Further, Crombie can be accused of begging the question in the following way. If it is asserted that Tom loves Mary then one can only ask 'Who is Tom?' if one already understands that 'Tom', in this use, is the proper name of some person. If one did not understand this one could not raise the question. The use of the personal pronoun 'who' here presupposes that 'Tom', in this use, is the proper name of a person.

Hence, I contend that Crombie's argument will not suffice and, in any case, it can well be denied that God is a person even on theological grounds; on the contrary, God is said to be three persons in one substance. Even though we are not told *what* that substance is and perhaps cannot in the nature of the case be so told, it is implied that the substance itself is not a person. Indeed, in cases where an attempt is made to say what that substance is, the answer is 'God', not person. What then is Crombie's case for saying that whilst 'God', in his view, satisfies one requirement for being a proper name, it does not satisfy the other (assuming that these requirements are exhaustive)? His case is that it is a necessary condition of any expression being a proper name that one can be brought into a situation in which it is proper to say 'That is A'; but one can never be brought into a situation in which it is proper to say 'That is God'. Now Crombie is correct on the point that if 'A' is the proper name of an object or person, then there is a conceivable situation in which one either could be or could have been brought face to face with the bearer of 'A' and be told: 'That X is A' (where 'X' is a general term which can supply at least a criterion of continued identity). But he is incorrect on the point

11

that if 'A' is the proper name of anything whatever then there is such a conceivable situation, for 'One' (e.g.) is the proper name of the number one[22] but there certainly seems to be no conceivable situation in which a person can be brought face to face with a number.

Thus, I contend, both Crombie's case for 'God' being a proper (proper) name and an improper (proper) name fail; in both cases his criteria are inadequate and in the first case the question is begged.

4. What then are the problems which arise for the thesis that 'God' is a proper name?

A. In order to speak of God as 'almighty', 'everlasting' and 'merciful', as in the prayers cited earlier, we should have to specify what sort of thing it is which is almighty, everlasting, etc., which is the bearer of the name 'God'. Not only is it impossible to raise this question if 'God' is a description, a general term, but if we *do* construe 'God' as a proper name, then it is impossible to answer this question (see below).

B. If we do construe 'God' as a proper name then we have to specify what the bearer of the name is and this is impossible. As Aquinas argues,[23] God is not in any genus; yet just this is required in order for us to begin to specify the bearer of the name. Aquinas' point, as I read it, is not that it is simply false that God is in any genus, but that 'He' could not in principle be so, for to so maintain that 'He' is, would be to maintain that there was something prior to God, which is a conceptually impossible position to maintain according to the principles of Christianity. Against this it might be pressed that:

   (1) on the contrary, 'God' is the proper name of some spirit, viz. that God is in the genus 'spirit'.
   (2) 'God' is the proper name of some person.
   (3) 'God' is the proper name of (simply) some being.
   (4) 'God' is the proper name of some transcendent being.

To consider (1). I surmise that the rationale for this view comes from St John's comment that God is (a) spirit but his comment need not be so construed; it could well be construed as 'Whatever has the nature of being God, has the nature of spirit'. Indeed, if we do construe 'spirit' as indicating the genus to

12

which God as an individual belongs, we are in dire difficulties. Mr Crombie, who has recently advocated this line of thought in the paper already referred to, has placed himself in just such difficulties. Crombie is concerned to 'fix the reference range' of theological statements, viz. supply an answer to the question 'What does 'God' refer to?' He presses the case that we need the conception of the divine and comments that even the harshest critics might be prepared to 'entertain the notion of a being outside space and time'.[24] Such a being he calls 'a spirit'. If then 'spirit' is to 'fix the reference range' of statements concerning God (where 'God' is a proper name even if in an 'improper' use), then 'spirit' must be able to supply the answer to the question 'What does 'God' refer to?', or, more correctly, the prior question 'What is 'God' the proper name of?' This latter question is prior since one cannot speak of the reference of 'God' if one does not know what the bearer of the proper name is and every genuine proper name must at some time have a bearer, though a name 'A' does not cease to be a proper name if it ceases to have a bearer. Yet on Crombie's own admittance, 'spirit' cannot supply an answer. He says:

> . . . the notion of spirit is, not exactly an illusion, but an illegitimate notion; illegitimate because it is a kind of reified abstraction. For the words 'spirit', 'spiritual' and so forth come to have a specific meaning for us by being connected with particular characteristics of, or events in, human beings . . . 'Spirit' derives from 'spiritual' and 'spiritual' acquires specific meaning by correlation with thinking and other activities which only occur, in our experience, as activities of human beings. 'Spirit', then, is not a common noun like 'mouse', because it is not the name of a distinctive kind of being: it follows from the way the specific meaning of the word is learnt that it is an abstract noun like 'digestion', because it stands for activities of beings called men.[25]

I concur with Crombie's remarks here. To speak of man as a spirit is simply to say that man is the subject of certain kinds of activities; it is not to say that he is or possesses some kind of immaterial substance. To say, that (e.g.) Socrates is a spirit is simply to say that the man Socrates is capable of carrying out and has carried out a certain range of activities. In Aristotelian

13

terms, man has the *form* spirit; Socrates (the individual man) has the *form* spirit, i.e. exhibits a certain kind of life. Rejection of the thesis that 'spirit' is a genus does not of course mean that St John's remark is to be regarded as nonsensical, only that it is not to be construed in this way.

To consider (2). This thesis runs into difficulties from the theological point of view, viz., from the doctrine of the Trinity, as I have already noted. But in any case it is in difficulties from a purely logical standpoint. To say that A is a person is not to say *what* A is, i.e. to allocate A to a certain class, but to allocate A to a category. It is to attribute a status to A where we already know the answer to the 'What is A?' question. In short, it allocates a status to an individual which *already* falls under a species and indicates to us what can be sensibly predicated of such an individual. It does not and cannot answer the question 'What is A?' where 'A' is the proper name of an individual; it is not, as St Augustine implies,[26] a genus of which man is a species. I have argued this case fully elsewhere and have not the space to reproduce it here.[27] Again, even if 'person', as I maintain, is a category term attributing a status to some individual already identified, then even if someone is tempted to say that God is a person, it does not follow that such a remark is in some way nonsensical, only that it cannot be construed as allocating God to a class – which is an impossible position to maintain in any case in the light of St Thomas's remark discussed earlier. Such a saying can be construed as 'Whatever is God is a person', even though this construction might bring difficulties in its train if there are difficulties for the case that 'God' is an ordinary descriptive predicable, as I shall later argue there are.[28]

To consider (3). This thesis is ruled out immediately on the grounds that there is no such class as the class of things which simply *are*, viz. 'beings' as such. It might be claimed that far from being a genuine insight of both Aristotle and Schopenhauer, this is a mere dogma and one cited by British philosophers when faced with the supposed extravaganzas of Continental Existential Philosophy and Theology. That it is no such mere dogma has been made clear to us by the development of modern formal logic, but lest anyone should be in any doubt, let him consider the following. The ability to answer the 'What-

14

is-it?' question (Aristotle's 'τi $\dot{\epsilon}\sigma\tau\iota$') of an individual demands that the answer so given can furnish a principle of identity for the individual. My telling you that there is simply a being in the corner of this room does not have the possibility of identifying anything for you. To so say would simply amount to saying that there is something (in the definite sense of 'something') in the corner and for you to *begin* to identify what I was going on to speak about, you would have to know at least some answer to the question 'Something – namely *what*?' To think that 'a being' can have the possibility of identifying an object is to confuse a 'formal' concept with a 'proper' one.[29] Again, 'thing' or 'being' cannot furnish us with a principle of individuation; to be told that there are two men in a room which have the 'property' of being 'beings' does not enable one to individuate the two individuals concerned. To think that it does is to engage in the error of treating 'being' as a property which things might have or fail to have – yet such things already have to *be* in order to have the supposed property. Finally, if 'being' is itself a class (the widest class that there is) then it would be possible to say 'There are such things as beings' or 'Beings exist', which would be pure nonsense. To put the matter crudely, the existential quantifier cannot quantify over itself.

To consider (4) If 'being' is not itself nor can be a genus, then it is quite misguided to think that 'transcendent being' can signify a species of being such that 'transcendent being' can answer the question posed. This is not, however, to say that the notion of 'transcendent being' is nonsensical or that we cannot say that God is a transcendent being without being open to the charge of engaging in some kind of logical fallacy. On the contrary, pointing out the above error clears the way for a more illuminating understanding of such remarks, namely as remarks of 'grammar' in Wittgenstein's sense.[30] To say that God is a transcendent being, far from answering the 'What is it?' question, places God in a category, not a class. It indicates to us what can sensibly be said of God, i.e. demarcates a universe of discourse. It indicates what predicates it is possible to use of God and hence determines what propositions are possible concerning God. For example, saying that God is a transcendent being rules out the following questions (for transcendent

15

entities transcend time), and from the status of propositions any remark formed from answers to those questions:

(i) When did God come into existence?
(ii) How long has God been in existence now?
(iii) When will God cease to exist?

The following remarks formed from answers to these questions are not possibly true or false as concerns God and hence not possible propositions concerning God:

(i) God came into existence at 4500 B.C.
(ii) God has been in existence nearly 7000 years now
(iii) God will cease to exist in A.D. 2000.

It is also worthwhile pointing out here that whilst another possible candidate for the post of answering the question 'What is "God" the proper name of?' is 'a supreme being' (which candidate is to be rejected for reasons offered above) this does not mean that to say that God is a supreme being is nonsense or in some other way an impossible remark to make. It only becomes impossible when it is used to answer the above question. Again, there is nothing problematical about such a remark if it is viewed as a 'grammatical' one, viz. a grammatical remark to the effect that God cannot sensibly be spoken of in certain ways (e.g. as coming into existence or going out of existence, as suffering change and decay, as being created or destroyed, as being in space or subject to space). A sceptic might raise the question as to why anything which can be so spoken of should be regarded as 'supreme'. In reply to this one must comment that there is the view that to be ungenerable, incorruptible, immutable, or eternal is to be 'better' than to possess the contrary 'formal' characteristics and that this way of thinking is present in our ordinary ways of thinking.[31] The only kind of rationale that can be put forward for such a way of thinking (if we are of the opinion that even common sense views and ways of speaking are in need of a rationale on the grounds that some common sense views, at any rate, have themselves been derived from Philosophy) is an argument to the effect that the very introduction of the notions of 'coming into existence/passing away', 'suffering change and decay', 'begin created/being destroyed', etc., suppose a reference to the concepts of 'that which eternally is', 'that which is immutable' and 'that which is

16

incorruptible'. Such an argument I have advocated in my paper 'St Thomas' Third Way'.[32]

C.   If we do construe 'God' as a proper name then the proposition 'God exists', in the sense of 'exists' represented by '$(\exists x)Fx$', is impossible, as the proposition 'Socrates exists' in this sense of 'exists' is impossible. To think that (e.g.) 'Socrates exists' is a possible proposition is to make the mistake of applying that which only applies to propositional functions to a value for an individual variable which occurs in a function. As Russell says:

> When you take any propositional function and assert of it that it is possible, that it is sometimes true, that gives you the fundamental meaning of 'existence'. You may express it by saying that there is at least one value of x for which that proposition function is true. Take 'x is a man', there is at least one value of x for which this is true. This is what one means by saying that 'There are men' or that 'Men exist'. Existence is essentially a property of a propositional function. . . . It is of propositional functions that you can assert or deny existence. You must not run away with the idea that this entails consequences which it does not entail. If I say 'The things that are in the world exist' that is a perfectly correct statement . . . But I must not go on to 'This is a thing in the world, and therefore this exists'. It is there the fallacy comes in, and it is simply, as you see, a fallacy of transferring to the individual which satisfies a propositional function a predicate which only applies to a propositional function.[33]

If it be contended that (e.g.) 'Socrates exists' is, after all, *pace* Quine, writable as 'There is an x such that x socratises', then we must charge the contender with making a radical confusion – i.e. that of construing a proper name as a 'mini' predicable. But, as Geach has well argued[34] a proper name is never a predicable – not even, one might add, a 'mini' one. This is not to say that (e.g. 'Socrates exists' is an impossible proposition for *any* sense of 'is'. It is perfectly possible in that sense of 'is' which Geach contends is Aquinas's sense of *esse*[35], but this is not the sense under discussion or the sense intended when it is asserted by Catholic Theology that God exists. It must be admitted that there are problems as to whether 'God

17

exists' is a possible proposition on some Christian conceptions of God, which such problems I shall be discussing later.[36] But these are *not* the problems which arise in connection with saying 'A exists' where 'A' is a proper name.

D.   Professor Geach[37] has used the argument that if 'God' were a proper name, then to say 'There are many Gods' would not merely be an untrue supposition but an unintelligible one. This is perfectly correct granted that 'God' is, as Geach maintains, an ordinary descriptive predicable term, for we can only prefix 'one', 'many', or 'several' to a general term and never to a proper name.[38]

E.   To refer to Geach again[39] if 'God' were a proper name, then 'God' would be transliterated into other languages, which is not the case. 'God' is translated into other languages – 'Θεός', '*Dieu*', '*Deus*'. Mr Robin Attfield has recently argued[40] that this point only establishes that 'God' is sometimes a common name rather than a proper name. His case for this is that 'if God is necessarily omnipotent there could not be more than one God, and it is not misleading to use 'God' as a proper name'. On the contrary, it is highly misleading. From the fact that either there is or even could be only one object satisfying a certain description, that description does not thereby become a name and to use it as a name is to radically confuse names and predicables.

F.   If 'God' were the proper name of some entity, then it would not be pertinent to ask of God what 'His' name is; it is not pertinent to ask for the name of an already named object. But this question is asked and answered in Holy Scripture, viz. '"Almighty" is His name' (Exodus 15.3. Cf. *Summa Theologica* Ia, q13, a3).[41]

G.   If 'God' were a proper name then it could only occur in the subject place of a subject-predicate proposition and never, by itself, in the predicate place. A proper name may occur as part of a predication but never as the whole predicate.[42] Yet it is at least *prima facie* plausible to hold that 'God' does so occur in the predicate place in such a proposition as 'Jesus Christ is God'. The proposition 'Jesus Christ is God' cannot be construed as a proposition of identity concerning two named individuals for in that case we should have to construe the proposition as propounding that the proper names 'Jesus Christ' and 'God' have one and the same bearer, which would

18

entail that Jesus Christ was identical with the Godhead, which is not Christian teaching.

H.   On the assumption that 'God' is a proper name, we should have to maintain that in order for 'God' to have any meaning,[43] i.e. to be a *genuine* proper name, there must currently be or have been some individual so named, viz. a bearer of the name. But there can be no individual so named and that individual be the Christian God, for God has no spatial, temporal, or spatio-temporal location and is not dependent for His identity upon reference to a spatio-temporal framework. Several comments are in place here.

First, it might be denied that in order for a proper name to have a sense or meaning it is necessary for there to be an entity so named, viz. a bearer of the name. What about proper names occurring in fiction? These have no bearers, yet surely they have a meaning? 'Wackford Squeers' is not a meaningless name like 'Floops'. Names occurring in fiction, however, are invented names for invented characters; they have a meaning in that we can specify what they pretendingly name in their use in the piece of fiction in which they occur. They do not purport to be genuine names. They have a pretended bearer, and a pretended reference on a token occasion of use, but no one would wish to claim that a pretended bearer or reference is a species of bearer or reference. Of course, one can ask (e.g.) 'To whom are you referring when you refer to Wackford Squeers?' and get the reply 'The character in Dickens' novel *Nicholas Nickleby* who ran a disgraceful educational establishment in the North Riding of Yorkshire', but to refer to a character in a novel is simply to refer to something someone has written. The identity of the character is uniquely determined by what the author writes and the existence of the character is the existence of what is written. On the contrary, the identity of the bearer or reference of a proper name in a given use is not at all determined by what someone happens to write about such a bearer; indeed, someone so writing presupposes such identity. Again, the existence of the bearer of an ordinary proper name is certainly not the existence of what is written about such a bearer; what is written about such a bearer presupposes the existence of the bearer at some time in order for what is said to be true or false. In contrast, what is written in

19

works of fiction cannot be said to be true or false, as opposed to (say) conveying a truth. If I say that Wackford Squeers killed Nicholas Nickleby this is only false in that Dickens did not say that he did. In any case, to bring up this purported difficulty about fictitious proper names would only be of value in the present context if anyone were to maintain that 'God' is such a name – a thesis which cannot be seriously entertained, for to so entertain it would entail maintaining that for God to exist would simply be for what is written about God to exist. Rush Rhees in considering the question of the way in which we learn the meaning of 'God', comments that it is not by having someone point and say '*That's* God' (implied: as it is with proper names). And in reply to the objection that we do not learn what 'Red Ridinghood' means by having anyone point either (the point of the objection being that the 'non-pointing' situation is not sufficient to show that 'God' is not a proper name), he further points out that the Red Ridinghood case is precisely *not* parallel to the God case, just because the former *is* a deliberate fiction:

> And to say that it is fiction is to say that the language is supposed to have the same *kinds* of meanings as the language about everyday things has. But the language about God is not fiction and is not understood as fiction.[44]

I concur with these remarks and have tried to bring out what one would be committed to if one construed 'God' as a fictitious proper name like 'Red Ridinghood'. The further point of value in Mr Rhees' comments is that it is misguided to think that to say (e.g.) 'God is merciful' is *like* saying (e.g.) 'Socrates is merciful' where 'Socrates' is the proper name of some man, but I shall not pursue this insight here.

Secondly, it is necessary to show that 'God' cannot be conceived of as the proper name of some spatio-temporal individual. Let us consider spatial predicates first. One cannot sensibly raise the question 'Where is God?' It might be denied that this is so and asserted that, on the contrary, God is in Heaven. This assertion however is void of content, for it is not logically possible that God should be 'anywhere' else than in Heaven if it is true that He is in Heaven. Indeed it might be pressed that if we raise the question 'Where is God?' and get the reply 'in Heaven', this is precisely to deny the validity of

20

the question. It is not merely false that Heaven is 'above the bright blue sky'; it could not possibly be so. This can be briefly seen as follows. If Heaven *were* a locatable region in space then it would make perfectly good sense for us to speak of 'going to Heaven in an old Ford car' or 'by rocket'. But such talk is clearly absurd – as is the claim that Heaven does not exist since otherwise astronauts would have discovered it or at the very least N.A.S.A. would have detected it. It is not possible that one could go to Heaven by an old Ford car, not simply because an old Ford car won't get that far, but because there is no place to go. As Our Lord said: 'The kingdom of Heaven is within you'. Further, if anyone replies that God occupies spatial position in that He is *everywhere*, they are guilty of a simple logical blunder, namely that of assuming that 'everywhere' is the name of the collection of all possible spatial locations. But 'everywhere' is not the name either of any given spatial location or of the collection of all possible spatial locations. If one considers propositions in which 'everywhere' has sensible employment this becomes clear:

(i) 'They seek him here, they seek him there, they seek him everywhere' (said of the Scarlet Pimpernel)

This is writable as: 'They seek him here, namely ——, they seek him there, namely ——, they seek him everywhere, namely —— (in all the cities of Europe)'. That is, for any use of 'everywhere' we must be able to supply a 'namely rider', namely in A, B, C . . . n. 'Everywhere' is simply the abstract form of the quantifier 'Every ——', where the blank is a general term introducing a class of places.

(ii) 'The Communist infiltrators are to be found everywhere nowadays'.

This has the form: 'The Communist infiltrators are to be found in every —— nowadays' and the propounder of such a proposition, if he is to talk sense, must be prepared to say what the value or values for the blank are in 'every ——'. All this, however, is *not* to say that if a Christian says that God is everywhere he is talking nonsense – only to say that the use of such a sentence cannot be either to (a) attribute a definite spatial position to God or (b) attribute a collection of spatial positions to God, such a collection being viewed as a whole. The sense in which

21

God is everywhere is something which, as far as I know, has yet to be worked out, though I think St Theresa knew the answer. Further, for any occupant of space, X, save for those occupants of space defined by their spatial position (if there are any so uniquely defined)[45] it is possible that at some time T_1, X is occupying spatial position A, whilst at time T_2 is occupying position B. However, it does not seem possible to say in connection with God that at any time T_1 God is at spatial position A, whilst at time T_2 God is at spatial position B – viz. to allocate a series of consecutive spatial positions to God in a given time series. Indeed, it might be pressed by the sceptical that it was precisely to get out of this difficulty that the dictum that God is everywhere was introduced. I think this latter point would be a sceptical view since the dictum that God is everywhere is not a thesis to get out of difficulties; if it *were* put forward to get out of this difficulty, it would land one in an absurdity. Finally, if 'God' is the proper name of a spatial occupant one could sensibly ask what *kind* of spatial occupant the bearer of the name is (e.g., two, three, or four dimensional), which strikes one as absurd. To allocate any given spatial position or series of spatial positions to God within a time series would be to commit, in part, that sin which Protestant Theologians (rightly) are always warning us against, namely that of making God a 'thing', 'one entity amongst many'.

I now consider temporal predicates. If 'God' is the proper name of a temporal entity, then one can sensibly ask the following questions:

(i) What position does God (continue) to occupy in our ordinary or any other temporal scheme, i.e. How long has God existed?

(ii) When did God come into existence?

(iii) When is it anticipated that God will cease to exist?

In reply to (i) it might be said that God occupies no definite period in any temporal scheme, unlike (e.g.) General de Gaulle. 'He' did not come into existence at any given moment of time (at any given point on some time scale); neither will he go out of existence at some future moment of time. 'He' has continuous existence; He came into existence at the first moment of time and will either (a) go out of existence at the last moment of time or (b) will continue in existence after time has ceased.

22

There seems to be several blunders in this reply, which reply gives rise to the picture of God as an old man with an exceedingly long beard, the length of the beard indicating the length of time God has been in existence. First, to say that God came into existence at the first moment of Time is not, as here envisaged, to specify a time at which anything could come into existence, for 'the first moment of Time' is a variable which takes as a value some particular time in a particular time scale and the question pertinent here is 'Which time scale?' Perhaps someone who advocated the 'Old Man' picture of God would reply that God came into existence at the first moment of time for any time scale whatsoever, but this contention is open to the charge that, since different types of entity occupy different time scales, God must be the subject of radically different and mutually exclusive predicates. Again, this contention assumes that 'the last moment in Time' itself designates some particular moment in time, whereas it calls for an interpretation and gives rise to problems parallel to those just raised. The formulation of the above position in terms of (b), viz. 'will continue in existence after time has ceased', is open to the charge of being a sure nonsense for the very notion of 'continuing in existence' supposes the operation of a time scale and that, whilst something which is in time can cease to exist, Time itself can neither come into existence or cease to exist; to suppose it can is to make the nonsensical assumption that Time itself is *in* time.

In spite of all this it might still be pressed that the question 'When did God come into existence?' is nevertheless a possible question to ask, though the question 'When will God cease to exist?' is not so possible. The former question is to be answered by 'in the beginning' and that God has existed *from* the beginning. Now it is certainly said that God has existed from the beginning and some have even said that God came into existence at the beginning of time, but whatever is intended to be conveyed by these remarks (and this I shall venture to comment on later), what *cannot* be being maintained is that 'in the beginning' answers the question posed – or if it *is* taken to answer this question, we have a sure nonsense on our hands. To say that God has existed from the beginning cannot be to say that there is some time T_1 since when God has existed, for 'the beginning' cannot itself designate a period or instant of time – not even a minute one. On the contrary, 'the beginning' indicates a *limit*. *If* Christian Theologians have thought of 'the beginning' as some definite time period or even an instant they have been seriously misguided. However, Christian Theologians are not necessarily open to the charge of speaking nonsense when they say that God has existed from the beginning, for an alternative account of this saying can be given. It has the role of showing that the question to which it is the putative answer is itself a nonsensical question, i.e. 'in the beginning' and 'from the beginning' being nonsensical answers to the questions 'When did God come into existence?' and 'How long has God existed?' The answers show the questions themselves to be nonsensical in the sense of impossible questions to ask from the standpoint of Christian Theology. Similarly, to answer the question 'When will God cease to exist?' by 'at the end of time' treats a terminus as itself an instant or period of time, engrosses one in a nonsense and this shows that the question itself is an impossible one to ask. It might be pressed that I have already treated the answer to the above question in terms of 'in (at) the beginning' too seriously, for such phrases are to be understood as 'in (at) the beginning *of time*' and it will rightly be argued that, whilst one can introduce 'the beginning' in relation to any given time period as indicating a limit of that time period, one cannot introduce 'the beginning' in relation to Time *itself*, without assuming that Time itself is a time period, which is an unintelligible assumption – and likewise in regard to 'the end of Time'. This further point further substantiates my point that 'at (in) the beginning' cannot possibly answer the original question and goes further to indicate that the original question cannot be raised and hence that 'God' cannot be regarded as the proper name of a temporal individual. I thus conclude that there are crucial objections to the thesis that 'God' is the proper name of a spatio-temporal individual.

Thirdly, it will be pointed out that the argument at the beginning of this section assumes that for 'God' to be a proper name, 'God' must be the proper name of a spatio-temporal individual, or at least a temporal individual, whereas (a) it is not necessary that if X is an individual that X be either a spatio-temporal individual or a temporal one (there can be non-spatio-temporal individuals) and (b) there can be proper names which are not the proper names of individuals.

Concerning (a) it might be said that '7' (the numeral) is the proper name of the number seven, yet numbers do not have existence in space/time nor require a reference to spatial ideas in order for their identity to be established, yet we can indeed produce criteria for the identity of numbers. Now, whilst it is the case that numbers do not exist in space and time, it is not the case, I shall contend, that they do not need a reference to the idea of spatial position in order for their identity to be established. The identity of a real number is uniquely determined by the position it occupies in a series, but the very idea of a series and that of position in a series necessarily involves at least an implicit reference to the idea of spatial position. This can be seen from the following passage taken from a textbook of mathematics:

> Consider a straight line that can be extended indefinitely in either direction. On this line choose a point 0 to represent zero and, using a suitable scale, mark off to the right one, two, three units, etc., to represent the positive numbers 1, 2, 3, etc., respectively. The negative numbers -1, -2, -3, etc., will be similarly marked to the left of 0 along this line.
>
> Any point on this line will represent a number according to the chosen scale, and any such number is known as a *real number*.[46]

The reference to spatial position is not, as first might be thought, a mere heuristic device. Frege has to have reference to it in his attempt to define the Number 1. He writes:[47]

> Therefore on our definition (§ 76), the Number which belongs to the concept "identical with o" follows in the series of natural numbers directly after o.
>
> Now if we give the following definition:
>
> 1 is the Number which belongs to the concept "identical with o", we can put the preceding conclusion thus:
>
> 1 follows in the series of natural numbers directly after o.

Now in § 76 Frege defines the relation in which every two adjacent members of the series of natural numbers stand to each other. He writes:

> The proposition:
> "there exists a concept F, and an object falling under it x, such that the Number which belongs to the concept F is n

25

and the Number which belongs to the concept 'falling under F but not identical with x' is *m*"

is to mean the same as

"*n* follows in the series of natural numbers directly after *m*"

but (i) in order to *begin* such a definition Frege has to understand the concept of 'adjacent members of a series' and (ii) in order for us to accept the definition we have to understand what it is for two objects to be identical, which in turn involves reference to the notion of spatial identity. On these grounds I contend that the existence of numbers is not a counter case to the thesis under consideration. There are, however, other candidates to be considered. Plato's 'Forms' are a case in point. It might be pressed that Plato thought that 'τὸ ἕν' was the proper name of an eternal individual, the proper name of the Form 'Unity'. If Plato did so think it is difficult to see how he could maintain that the form 'Unity' could be 'present in' many individuals called 'one', for a name cannot have instantiation or application. Even if we do, for present purposes, grant that Plato wanted 'τὸ ἕν' as (i) the proper name of the Form 'Unity' and (ii) as the predicable 'one'[48] there seem to be insuperable difficulties in maintaining that ' τὸ ἕν' is the proper name of an eternal individual, for the problem arises how it is possible to uniquely individuate such a supposed individual. It might be contended that the individual Form 'Unity' can be uniquely individuated from other Forms in Plato's ontology by such considerations as (a) the position it occupies in the hierarchy of Forms and (b) what can sensibly be said of this Form as opposed to other Forms in the same class in Plato's hierarchy.

But such a differentiating procedure can only supply us with differentia for *types* of Form, not with differentia for an individual Form. The moral of this is that, even if 'τὸ ἕν', etc., are regardable as proper names of eternal entities, they can only be so regardable as proper names of types, not as proper names of individuals, so we do not have a case for saying that Plato's Forms are cases of non spatio-temporal individuals which are the bearers of proper names. Someone might also claim that such entities as thoughts or intentions are cases of non-spatio-temporal individuals, but whilst such entities are not in space or time, they require a reference to space and time for their identification since they are identified by reference to the human beings whose thoughts and intentions they are.

On (b) above it will be pressed that there are proper names of types as well as individuals. 'Gold' (e.g.) is the proper name of a type of metal, similarly 'Iron', and 'Man' is the proper name of a species of animal. Upon investigation however, this turns out to be an illusion. For 'Gold', etc., to be the proper names of types, it is supposed that 'Gold', etc., are proper names in the first place. Yet to so suppose is to be guilty of a confusion. For any proposition in which 'Gold' (e.g.) occurs as a putative logical subject, purporting, we might suppose, to name some metal, we cannot construe it as such. Such propositions are always writable in the form:

'Whatever is gold is . . .';

'Gold' only has the appearance of the proper name of some type; in truth it is simply the verbal expression of the 'concept'[49], the predicable, 'gold' written with a capital letter to meet the requirements of style. It does not thereby change its essential predicative nature.[50]

I. If 'God' is a proper name, then on a given occasion of use of the word 'God', it must make sense to ask what the reference of the name is. But the question of reference here makes no sense, for, as I have previously argued, and as has often been said, God is 'outside space and time'; yet the very notion of 'referring' has a necessary reference to either a temporal, or spatial or spatio-temporal scheme. One can only refer in such a scheme or to entities which depend for their identity upon reference to individuals in such a scheme (e.g. thoughts, feelings, intentions are such dependent entities). However, it is clear that it is impossible to refer to God in the way in which one refers to such non-substantial entities as thoughts or intentions, for such non-substantial entities are dependent for their identity and existence on substances by reference to which they are identified (and identifiable) and hence referred to; whereas God, it is claimed, is dependent upon nothing else for His identity or existence.

J. On the assumption that 'God' is a proper name, it is difficult to cope with the traditional Catholic view of Theology as a science (*Summa Theologica* Ia, q2, a1) for a science in this (Aristotelian) sense deals not, save *per accidens*, with 'individual

27

facts'[51] but with 'universal facts', i.e. with universal propositions which are necessarily true.[52]

In the light of the above considerations it is my claim that 'God' cannot be taken to have the status of a proper name in Christian writing and hence that one case for saying that sentences of the form: 'God is F', as introduced at the beginning of this chapter, can be construed as expressing propositions of a subject–predicate type, falls to the ground.

2 On Whether 'God', if not a Proper Name, Can Introduce a Subject of Predication

Having rejected the contention that 'God' is a proper name such that we have a *prima facie* case for saying that sentences of the form 'God is F' express propositions of a subject–predicate kind, it will be contended that it by no means follows that 'God' cannot stand as a logical subject (introduce a subject of predication), for whilst it is a sufficient condition of 'A' potentially occurring as introducing a subject of predication that 'A' is a proper name, it is not a necessary one; some definite descriptions (e.g.) can so occur. It might be pressed that there is a *prima facie* case for saying that 'God' is an abbreviated definite description of the form 'The one and only F'. It might further be claimed that, despite certain difficulties[1], 'God' is an abbreviated definite description of the form 'The God of ——', where the blank can be filled out with a proper name so that we have as examples 'The God of Israel' and 'The God of Abraham, Isaac and Jacob'. These two accounts do not lead to inconsistency; it might be true both that A is the one and only God and that A is the God of Israel. Professor Strawson holds, *contra* Russell, that definite descriptions of the latter form can certainly stand as introducing subjects of predication, i.e. stand as logical subjects, though not those of the former. Descriptions of the latter form he designates 'referring expressions', though the class of such expressions is wider than the class of such descriptions and he characterises the class of such expressions as expressions which can be used to make identifying reference to a particular.[2] Such expressions can serve to introduce subjects of predication and proper names are only one class of such expressions. 'Expressions of these kinds include some proper names, some proper nouns, some descriptive phrases beginning with the definite article and expressions compounded of these.[3]

29

My plan of campaign for this chapter is as follows:

A. (1) I shall first argue that Strawson's argument in 'On Referring' in favour of descriptive phrases of the form 'The so and so' standing as logical subjects is open to fatal objections.

(2) But that from the fact that definite descriptions of a certain form cannot be said either to gain their meaning (sense) or have their meaning (sense) in that they have a certain use in Strawson's sense of use, it does not follow that such definite descriptions cannot stand as logical subjects, i.e. cannot introduce subjects of predication. The problem thus arises as to whether 'God' construed as such a description can so stand.

B. Granted that the Russellian analysis holds for propositions of the form 'The one and only —— is F' (which Strawson would not wish to dispute), I shall then raise the question of whether there are any difficulties for the thesis that 'God' is a definite description of the form 'The one and only F' such that sentences of the form 'The one and only God is F' can be said to express propositions of the form: ($\exists$x) (Gx and for all y, Gy only if y = x. Fx).

C. Even if it is rejected that 'God' is a definite description of either of the above forms, it might still be maintained that 'God' is a general term of a substantival kind in Professor Geach's sense.[4] Hence I shall raise the question of whether 'God', construed as such a kind of term, can stand as a logical subject.

A. My case against Strawson is as follows. His account of the meaning of a 'referring expression', i.e. an expression of the form 'The so and so' in terms of its use, is viciously circular. He writes:

> To give the meaning of an expression (in the sense in which I am using the word) is to give the *general directions* for its use to refer to or mention particular objects or persons ('On Referring')[5].

On Strawson's account an expression of the form 'The so and so' has a meaning in that it has a use and comes to have a meaning in that on some occasions it can be used to refer, even though it need not succeed in referring on every occasion of use. But in order to give such general directions for its use to mention or refer to particular objects or persons, I must first understand the meaning of the expression (otherwise I could never begin to decide that I had either succeeded or failed in mentioning or referring and indeed, I could not even begin to issue such general directions)[6]. And in order to give such general directions for the use of such an expression, I must first understand as well, not solely the verbal meaning of the expression, but also what it is for that expression *qua* description to have possible application, i.e. what it would be for something to satisfy that description. That is, a condition of my being able to give general directions for the referring use of such an expression as (e.g.) 'The present Queen of England' is that I first understand what it is for someone or other to be the present Queen of England. If I do not know what could possibly constitute satisfaction of this description I could not begin to use the expression to refer since I would have no idea what could possibly constitute a reference. In other words, a condition of setting out Strawson's general directions for the use of 'referring expressions' is that one already understands the predicative use of such definite descriptive phrases, i.e. we already have to understand their role as definite descriptions. Thus, Strawson's claim, that definite descriptions of a certain type can stand as logical subjects on the grounds that they both get their meaning from their referential function and have their meaning in that they have a referential function, fails.

We are now faced with the question 'Granted that descriptive phrases of the form above considered (definite descriptions of the form above considered) cannot be said to have meaning in that they have a referring or mentioning use, does it follow from this that they cannot have such a referring or mentioning use such that such expressions cannot stand as logical subjects?' Not at all. Such expressions cannot be said to have their sense from so standing, but this does not put a logical bar on such expressions so standing as logical subjects, for it can indeed be argued that for an expression to be a subject introducing one, it is not necessary that it gains its sense or has its sense in that it names or stands for anything. A definite description of the type under consideration can introduce a subject of predication (can stand as a logical subject) in that such definite descriptions (such definite descriptive phrases) are indeed used for the purpose of identifying objects (have the role of identifying objects) and an

31

expression which can be so used (have such a role) in being so used (in having such a role) is occurring as a logical subject. It introduces a subject of predication.[7] Not only do such definite descriptions have such a role, but Strawson goes so far as to claim that it is the prerogative of such definite descriptions to have such a role.[8] Now, whilst it cannot be denied with any degree of plausibility that such definite descriptions both can and do have such a role, *and* that it is the prerogative of such definite descriptions to play such a role, it must not be inferred from these considerations that such a role is the *primary* role of such descriptions. Such a role is essentially secondary since a condition of such definite descriptions being able to identify an object is that such descriptions are satisfiable, and, in order for such descriptions to succeed in identifying an object, there must be one such object which is satisfied by them. In other words identification presupposes description, but the consideration that the identificatory role is secondary does not exclude such a role.

Having allowed therefore that definite descriptions of the form 'The so and so' can occur as logical subjects in that they can identify objects for us about which we can then go on to make true or false predications, can such definite descriptions as 'The God of Israel' or 'The God of Abraham, Isaac and Jacob' so stand so that after all one can say that sentences of the form 'God is F' (where 'God' is an abbreviation for such a description) can express propositions of a subject–predicate kind? The answer to this seems to be in the negative. Strawson writes:

> But what exactly is this task of identifying an object for a hearer? Well, let us consider that in any communication situation a hearer (an audience) is antecedently equipped with a certain amount of knowledge, with certain presumptions, with a certain range of current perception. There are within the scope of his knowledge or present perception objects which he is able *in one way or another* to distinguish for himself. The identificatory task of *one* of the terms in predications of the kind we are now concerned with, is to bring it about that the hearer knows *which* object it is, of all the objects within the hearer's scope of knowledge or presumption, that the *other* term is being applied to. . . . That term (i.e. the definite singular term)[9] achieves its identificatory

32

purpose by drawing upon what in the widest sense might be called the conditions of its utterance, *including* what the hearer is presumed to know or to presume already, or to be in a position then and there to perceive for himself. . . . The possibility of identification in the relevant sense exists only for an audience antecedently equipped with knowledge or presumptions, or placed in a position of possible perception which he can draw on in this way.[10]

Can 'The God of Israel' perform such an identificatory function? Clearly it cannot meet Strawson's requirements for identification in a perceptual situation for to do so would require that God be a perceptual particular, which He is not. It is further the case that it cannot meet Strawson's requirements for a non-perceptual situation for Strawson's requirements concerning 'scope of knowledge or presumption' are introduced to cover those situations in which we make identifying reference to an object not immediately present to our perception but perceptible. Even if we allow that Strawson's stringencies regarding 'scope of knowledge or presumption' are introduced to cover not only non-present but nevertheless perceptible particulars, but also non-perceptible particulars, it is still not the case that 'The God of Israel' can perform such an identificatory role since for this term to perform such a role the term 'God' must be such as to introduce a class of either spatio-temporal particulars or temporal particulars or particulars dependent for their identification upon such particulars. I have already argued that God cannot be regarded as such a spatio-temporal particular; in so far as God can be regarded as exhibiting those formal characteristics ('internal properties' in Wittgenstein's sense) which other members of the class of Gods possess, 'Gods' does not introduce a class of spatio-temporal particulars and so descriptions of the form 'The God of ——' cannot perform such an identificatory role. If it be countered that the Gods *are*, after all, very special kinds of spatio-temporal particulars, then of course descriptions of the form 'The God of ——' can perform such an identificatory function, save where the blank is filled out by one or more of a particular range of names, i.e. those purportedly designating the God of Israel. Such a description as 'The God of Israel' can only be thought to have that identificatory function necessary to singular terms

33

if it is thought that Gods are either spatio-temporal particulars or have a necessary reference to such particulars for their identification or are in some way analogous to such particulars, which is not the case in that Gods are thought to be eternal, a-spatial entities. Thus such a description as 'The God of Israel' can only have the appearance of performing an identificatory role since the requirements which must be met in order for such an identificatory role to be possible cannot be met without making Gods items within our spatio-temporal framework or in some way items analogous to particulars within that framework. However, it is not possible for such an analogy to be drawn for there are not two sorts of particulars, (a) spatio-temporal ones or temporal ones or those dependent for their identification upon such particulars (such as thoughts, wishes, intentions) and (b) eternal particulars. Such supposed 'eternal particulars' can be no particulars at all, since even if we could specify what they are, we cannot individuate them and hence identify them.[11] I thus conclude that such a definite description as 'The God of Israel' cannot stand as a logical subject; that it is only by treating God, in particular, and Gods, in general, *as if they were* items within our spatio-temporal scheme, or dependent upon or analogous to such items, which *could* be identified by such singular terms of the form 'The so and so', as items within that scheme can, that such a role has been thought possible for such a description, and hence that sentences of the form 'God is F' can express propositions of a subject–predicate kind, where 'God' is an abbreviation for such a descriptive phrase.

B. It might now be contended that 'God' is not an abbreviation for a definite description of the form 'The God of ——', but for the definite description 'The one and only God'. If we thus take 'God', then sentences of the form 'God is F' certainly cannot be thought of as expressing propositions of a subject–predicate kind. As Strawson rightly comments:

. . . in the analysis of singular descriptions given in the Theory of Descriptions the identificatory function of singular terms is suppressed altogether. Its place is taken by an explicit assertion to the effect that there is just one thing with a certain property. But to say this is to do something quite different

34

from identifying that thing for a hearer in the sense I have been concerned with. One who says that there exists just one thing with a certain property typically intends to inform his hearer of this fact.[12]

Granted the Russellian analysis holds for propositions of the form 'The one and only —— is F', can we say that 'God' is such a definite description such that sentences of the form 'God is F' express a proposition of the form $(\exists x)$ (Gx and for all y, Gy only if y = x . Fx)? The answer unfortunately seems to be in the negative since for such a form of proposition to be expressed, even allowing that there are no inherent difficulties to be met in Russell's notion of an 'essentially undetermined variable "x"'[13] we should further have to allow that (a) there can be eternal, a-spatial individuals which the undeterminable variable 'x' can be said to range over, and (b) 'God' is at least an ordinary descriptive predicable term. That there can be no such eternal, a-spatial individuals I have already indicated and I shall further argue in favour of this thesis in my next chapter. As regards (b), in the last chapter I put forward considerations of the view that 'God' is such a term; I shall be raising difficulties for such a view in my next.

C. The above discussions have been based upon the contentions that 'God' is either an abbreviation for a definite description of the form 'The God of ——' or of the form 'The one and only F', but it might well be contended at this point that (a) 'God' is not such an abbreviation of either form, (b) that 'God' is a general term of a type which can stand as a subject of predication. That a certain type of general term can stand as a logical subject has recently been argued by Professor Geach in *Reference and Generality*. Geach argues that certain general terms can occur as names, those which he designates as 'substantival'.[14] Such general terms, he claims, can occur as the subjects of propositions though, of course, we have to have a criterion by which we can distinguish cases in which such substantival general terms are occurring as names from those in which such terms occur as a predicable. What then decides whether a general term is a substantival one, and is 'God' such a term? The criterion for substantivality is whether it makes sense to prefix the words 'the same' to a general term; this is on the

35

basis that when the same name is used in two acts of naming we can always ask whether the same thing is named. Now, granted that there are no difficulties for the thesis that 'God' is at least a general term, it does seem that 'God' is a substantival general term by such a criterion, for it certainly seems possible to say:

(i) The Christians do not worship the same God as the Mohammedans do
(ii) The Christians do worship the same God as the ancient Hebrews did

But even if 'God' can be said to be a substantival general term by this criterion, it does not follow that 'God' can stand as a logical subject unless Geach can show that any such general term can so occur. It is my case that, whilst it is true that when the same name is used in two acts of naming we can always ask whether the same thing is named, it does not follow from this that such general terms as can be substituted for 'thing' in 'the same thing is named' can occur as a name and hence as a subject of predication. For example:

(i) Socrates loved Xanthippe
(ii) Socrates twisted people with sincere moral beliefs into impossible logical positions by sophistical arguments

Here we have the same name, 'Socrates', being used in two acts of naming (in Geach's sense) and we can, indeed we have to, ask whether the same thing is being named in order to begin to decide whether these propositions are true or false. But one must not confuse the answer to the question 'Is the same thing being named by these two occurrences of the name "Socrates"?', which might take as its answer 'Yes, the same name "Socrates" names one and the same man, the philosopher who lived in fifth-century Athens, who was the teacher of Plato, etc.,' *with* a name, i.e. one must not confuse the specification of what is named with a name. An expression of the form 'the same ——' where the blank takes a general term is indeed needed for A to have the use of a proper name, but neither from this nor the parallel consideration above does it follow that such a general term can occur as a name. It certainly seems that Geach has moved from (a) stating a necessary requirement for the continued use of a name to (b) maintaining the thesis that any general term which can supply a criterion of identity for the continued use of a name A can itself occur as a name, which is to maintain, without further reasoning, that a condition for the use of a name is itself a name or, at the very least, can occur as a name. Without further reasoning it is not at all clear why this should follow and indeed it only follows on a confusion.

Geach, however, has a further argument. He writes:

> However, as I shall try to show, it is plausible to suggest that general terms (substantival ones, that is) also admit of such use as logical subjects. Indeed although the use of proper names in that capacity is much more easily recognised it is arguable that such use depends on the possibility of general terms also being logical subjects.[15]

What is his case for this? He begins his argument by commenting:

> For every proper name there is a corresponding use of a common noun preceded by 'the same' to express what requirements as to identity the proper name conveys: 'Cleopatra's Needle' – 'the same (bit of) stone'; 'Jemima' – 'the same cat' . . . In all these cases we may say that the proper name conveys a *nominal essence*; thus 'cat' expresses the nominal essence of the thing we call Jemima. . . .

With this I am not in dispute; it brings out the point that a condition of employing proper names for objects is that such objects must be of a certain sort or kind and that for a proper name to have a continued use we must be prepared to say that it names the same *x* on different occasions of use. The heart of Geach's argument is contained in the following paragraph:

> I might tell a story involving Jemima and the river Thames without using either of these proper names; I might refer to Jemima as 'a cat' and the Thames as 'a river' when I first mentioned them, and thereafter speak of 'the cat' and 'the river' – sc. 'the same cat' and 'the same river'. A hearer unacquainted even by hearsay with Jemima and the Thames would lose absolutely nothing by this suppression of the proper names. So if 'cat' in this story telling did not retain the use of a logical subject, how could 'Jemima' have such a

37

use? How could we make out that 'Jemima' has what it takes to be a logical subject, but 'cat' has not?[16]

Now whilst in the context of a story 'a hearer unacquainted even by hearsay with Jemima and the Thames would lose absolutely nothing by the suppression of the proper names' since in a story the question of *which* cat or *which* river would not arise, such a question might well do so and could always in theory do so in a non-story telling context. Even in a non-story telling context, however, it might be urged, nothing is lost by the *mere* suppression of the proper names. Agreed, nothing is lost by the *mere* suppression of the proper names but something *is* lost if all we introduce in lieu of such proper names is 'a cat' and 'a river' (sc. 'the same cat' and 'the same river'), for in a non-story telling situation, if we are faced with a purportedly true proposition 'A cat fell into a river', where 'a cat' is interpretable as 'a definite cat', viz. 'some cat' in the definite sense of 'some' and 'a river' as 'a definite river', viz. 'some river' in the definite sense of 'some', then the questions 'Which cat?' and 'Which river?' certainly arise and seek an answer either in terms of a definite description which can perform the role of uniquely identifying the cat or river or the proper name of the cat or river so identified. What then can putatively stand as a logical subject is either a definite description of a kind which can perform an identifying role or a proper name. All Geach's argument indicates is that definite descriptions of such a kind can stand as logical subjects, not that a certain kind of general term can. His case for saying that some general terms can (here) relies on the story-telling situation where the question 'Which one?' need not necessarily arise, though of course it could do so if his story about a cat and a river formed part of a collection of stories in which a number of cats and rivers were introduced. Geach's case would only hold if someone introduced the proposition 'Some cat fell into some river' where we had the indefinite sense of 'some', i.e. 'Some cat or other fell into some river or other'. Here, *ex hypothesi* the question 'Which one?' cannot arise and I am sure Geach would not wish to say that either 'cat' or 'river' in such a proposition was occurring as a logical subject. In sum, whilst Geach's point that proper names convey a nominal essence is perfectly correct, he has not shown that it follows from this that such 'nominal essences'

38

themselves must be able to stand as logical subjects. Thus, even if 'God', by Geach's criterion, is a substantival general term and hence might express the nominal essence of something or other, it does not follow that 'God' can occur as a logical subject.

It might be contended that even if Geach's argument fails, nevertheless it is plausible to hold that such general terms as he designates 'substantival' can stand as the subject of predication. To so plausibly hold demands that some additional argument be produced: in the absence of some such argument I concur with Frege's case that 'concepts' can never stand as logical subjects.[17] Concerning 'All mammals have red blood' he writes: 'We cannot fail to recognise the predicative nature of the concept "mammal"'.[18] We cannot say that 'mammals', even as so occurring 'stands for an object', i.e. 'mammals' is not the 'sign for an object'. Frege thus renders 'All mammals have red blood' as: 'If anything is a mammal then it has red blood.'[19] Now it can indeed be argued that this account is unsatisfactory for all occurrences of 'All mammals have red blood'. It will suffice for 'All mammals have red blood' for the reading 'Any mammal has red blood' and for the reading 'Every mammal has red blood', where this is the equivalent of 'Whatever is a mammal . . .', but not for 'Each and every mammal has red blood' for the reason that the hypothetical 'If anything is a mammal, then it has red blood', neither entails nor presupposes the existence of mammals. However, even though we must grant that for some readings of 'All mammals have red blood', we have 'Each and every mammal has red blood' such that for 'Each and every mammal . . .' we must write the names of the species of mammal, i.e. 'Men, horses, cows . . . have red blood', this does not show that a concept can stand as a logical subject. In such writings we indeed have concept words occurring as putative subjects but it is a mistake to think that such words do introduce subjects of predication: 'Men, horses, cows, whales . . . have red blood' for some readings can be expressed as 'Whatever is a man, horse, etc., . . . has red blood' or 'If anything is a man, horse . . . has red blood' and where such an expression is not possible, i.e. where we have 'Each and every man, horse, whale etc. . . .', such propositions are exponible as propositions expressing true predications concerning each and every member of the class mentioned. Thus, 'Each and every

39

man has red blood' is exponible as 'A, B, C, D . . . has red blood', where 'A', etc., are the proper names of individual men. Thus, what properly stands as the subject of the predication is the individual or a set of individuals, not, in Frege's terms, a concept. From the fact that we can rightly substitute for 'Each and every F is . . .' a proposition containing the names of each and every F, which proposition itself can be genuinely construed as of a subject–predicate type, it certainly does not follow that the original proposition is of such a type; indeed it would only be on a confusion that one could think it of such a type.

Throughout the latter part of this chapter I have worked on the assumption that 'God' is at the least an ordinary general term (Frege's *Begriffswort*) and at the most a general term of Geach's substantival type and in some of my earlier discussions in Chapter 1 I explicitly contended at least the minimal thesis. Just this assumption and contention may be objected to and it is to such objections that I turn in my next chapter.

3 On Whether 'God' is a Descriptive Predicable Term

As I commented in the last chapter, it seems that 'God' is not only an ordinary general term, a descriptive predicable term (Frege's *Begriffswort*), but also a substantival one by Geach's criterion since it does seem to make clear sense to prefix 'the same' to 'God' and to so sensibly prefix it it is not necessary to introduce some *other* term, as it is in the case of adjectival general terms (e.g. 'red'), which such other term would furnish us with a criterion of continued identity in Geach's sense. What then are the supposed difficulties in holding that 'God' is a descriptive predicable term?

1. Potential difficulties can be listed as follows:

(1) It might be said that to so construe 'God' is to confuse 'God' (with a capital 'G') with 'god' (with a small 'g'). The former cannot be prefaced by an indefinite article, the latter clearly can.
(2) 'God', as opposed to 'god' has no plural form; 'gods' is the plural of 'god' not 'God'.
(3) 'God', as opposed to 'god' is not enumerable: we can talk of 'one (many) god(s)' but not 'one (many) God(s)'. It follows from this that 'God' cannot sensibly be prefaced by 'the one and only'; only 'god' can be so prefaced and we cannot write for 'God', 'the one and only god', for God is not *a* god at all.
(4) If 'God' were a descriptive predicable term like 'man', as has been suggested, then it will, when being predicated of several individuals to form a putatively true proposition, naturally take the plural form, which places us in the position of having to say that in the conjoint proposition 'The Father is God and The Son is God and The Holy Spirit is God', we have to admit of three Gods, for on such a construction of 'God' the respective parts of such a proposition cannot be construed as propositions of identity.

41

(5) If 'God' were such then it would signify a genus, which is certainly contrary to the teaching of Aquinas (*Summa Theologica* Ia, q3, a5).

(6) On such a construction no place could be given to those assertions to the effect that God is a supreme being, or the supreme being, or even 'being itself'. On such a construction 'God' would simply be writable as 'a God' or at the most 'The one and only God'.

(7) On such a construction the proposition 'God exists'; '($\exists$x)Gx' would be possible; whereas, on the contrary, such a proposition is impossible – 'God does not exist; He is eternal'.

(8) It cannot be said that in a proposition of the form 'God is F' (where this is a subject–predicate form) we have a general term occurring in the subject place, for in the case of a general term thus occurring we do not have a single word but a word preceded by the indefinite article. For example, if we wish to make 'man' the subject of the subject–predicate proposition 'Socrates is a man', where 'man' is the predicate term, we have the form 'A man is Socrates' which is renderable as 'A man socratises' or 'A man has the property of being a socrates', *not* 'Man has the properties of being socrates' or 'Man socratises', which is what we have by parallel in the 'God' case.

(9) If 'God' were an ordinary descriptive predicable term, then God would be an ordinary 'Form' in Aquinas's sense[1]; but God is not such an ordinary Form in his sense, for 'ordinary' forms can be received in matter and are individuated by matter. God, however, is *not* a Form which can be 'received in matter' or be 'received by many' for God is a self-subsisting Form and is individualised precisely because it cannot be 'received in' a subject (*Summa Theologica* Ia, q3, a2 reply to objection 3).

(10) Far from it being the case that 'God' is a descriptive predicable term able to be precursed by a number or the indefinite article, 'God' is an abstract term, grammatically speaking an abstract noun. Common nouns, save when they occur at the beginning of sentences, do not take an initial capital letter, yet, since proper names are not translatable as between languages, 'God' is not of course a proper name. Abstract nouns however *are* translatable as between languages and they can and sometimes do occur with an initial capital letter when they are not occurring at the beginning of sentences; and 'God' exhibits such features.

2. I shall now comment on the above difficulties in detail.

(1) Certainly we must not confuse 'God' and 'god'. That is we must not confuse the concepts introduced by those respective items, for the concepts introduced by 'God' and 'god' do not, to coin a term from Wittgenstein, exhibit the same 'grammar'. As I have argued earlier, it does not make sense to attribute a spatial position to God; whatever is God is necessarily non-spatial. On the contrary the gods that Professor Geach mentions, i.e. Woden, Thor (in *God and the Soul*, p. 109), were such that it made sense to ask for their location, even though it is false that they do occupy any such location. The same goes for the Greek gods Geach alludes to in 'Form and Existence';[2] they were supposed to inhabit the top of Mount Olympus. Again, as I have argued earlier, God is eternal. 'He' is not an occupant of time, 'He' does not have continuous existence through time; on the contrary, the Greek gods, as Geach remarks, 'ever are' (*aeon ontes*). *They* can be said to come into existence, exist now (at any given time) and go on existing. It makes sense to say of them that they might cease to exist; it is simply held by believers in such entities that it is false that they ever will. We might say that the Greek gods are the example *par excellence* of temporal existents, but whatever is the Christian God is not so, and this, I contend, is brought out in the revelation that God is Alpha and Omega.[3] As Professor Malcolm has pointed out,[4] God necessarily exists; 'necessary existence' indicates an 'internal' property of whatever is God, an 'internal' property in Wittgenstein's sense (*Tractatus* 2. 01231). This is not to be confused with saying that it is necessary that God exists; an argument might be devised or have been produced having as its conclusion '[Therefore] it is necessary that God exists', but this of course does not entail that God's existence is necessary. It is only by an operator shift, parallel to what Dr Kenny calls a 'quantifier shift',[5] that such a supposed entailment could be reached. It has been said that since 'existence' is not a 'predicate', 'necessary existence' cannot be, and that therefore 'necessary existence' cannot indicate an 'internal' property of God. It seems to me that the proponents of such a position are confused since they assume that 'necessary existence' as appertaining to God is able to be split up logically into two elements 'necessary' and 'existence', when it is an unanalysable whole.

43

They would have to say that 'God necessarily exists' is exponible as 'God is necessary' and 'God exists' whereas the first proposition in the proposed analysis is an impossible one, since the question 'For what?', in this context, makes no sense. Further, such proponents assume that if it is asserted that God necessarily exists, then it is being assumed that 'exists' is functioning as a predicate, which is precisely to misconstrue the grammar of the remark.

To confuse 'God' and 'god' gets one into the position of having to say that when the Heathen says that his idol is god or the Thor worshipper that Thor is god and the missionary that the idol is not God or that Thor is not God, then missionary *contradicts* the worshipper of these entities, as Professor Geach says the missionary so does.[6] My worry over this line of thought is as follows. If the missionary is to be thought to be contradicting the idol worshipper or the Thor worshipper then he must be construed as saying that it is simply false that the idol or Thor is God, which gives rise to at least the following problems:

(a) If it is actually false that the idol or Thor is God, this presupposes that it is possibly false that such entities are God; but if it is possibly false that such entities are God then it is possibly true that such entities are God. However it is arguable, and I have attempted to so argue above, that it is not possibly true or false that such entities are God in the Christian sense, for 'god' and 'God' exhibit different 'grammars'.

(b) On this account all that could be maintained by the missionary or the Christian is that it is false that the idol or Thor is God, not, as is maintained, that these entities are *no* God, as opposed to merely false Gods.[7] Such entities are no God since they cannot, in their worshipper's conception of them, exhibit those 'internal' properties which God exhibits (e.g. eternity, a-spatiality, immutability, immortality).

From the consideration that we must not confuse 'God' and 'god' and that, as some Protestant theologians say, God is not *a god*, it does not follow that 'God' cannot be prefixed by the indefinite article, has no plural, or cannot be prefixed by 'one' or 'many' as maintained in objections (1)–(3) above. In order for such a position to be maintained some extra argument will have to be produced such that it can be shown

44

that 'God' as an item of Christian language cannot be so pre-cursed or added to. Further, even if it can be shown that 'God', as an item of Christian language cannot be so precursed or added to, it does not follow that 'God' is *not* a descriptive predicable term, *only* that it is not a descriptive predicable term of a certain type, i.e. one that can supply us with a unit of counting, but it is not a necessary condition of 'F' being a descriptive predicable term that 'F' can be so used. Aristotelian 'matter' terms and Quine's 'mass' terms cannot be so prefixed or added to but they are nevertheless descriptive predicable terms. Thus the question of whether 'God', as an item of Christian discourse, is a descriptive predicable term in either the sense of a 'count' term or a 'mass' term is still an open question.[8]

Again, objection (4) does not show that either: (a) 'God' cannot have a plural form 'Gods' or cannot sensibly be prefaced by 'one' or 'many' or (b) that 'God' is not a descriptive predicable term, since the argument here that 'God' cannot have a plural form is based upon a supposed problem for the doctrine of the Trinity if it does so admit of the plural form. But it could still hold true that 'God' does admit of the plural form (and hence of the singular), that there could be many individuals answering this description (though it is false that there are) and the doctrine of the Trinity remain unscathed on the grounds that in this case, 'The Father', 'The Son' and 'The Holy Spirit' are all either (a) names of aspects of one and the same individual or (b) descriptions of aspects of one and the same individual which such individual uniquely satisfies the description 'God', granted (i) the possibility of non-spatio-temporally determined individuals[9] and (ii) that 'aspect' is a term which can take a number in its own right.[10]

Objection (5) relies on the thesis that 'God is not in any genus' but from the truth of this thesis it does not follow that 'God' does not 'signify a genus'. What Aquinas argues is that God is not *in* any genus, not that 'God' does not signify a genus. God is not 'in' a genus either as a species or as 'being reducible to it' as e.g. a point and unity are reducible to the genus of quantity, but from this it does not follow that God is not a genus. Even so, there is still something of worth in this objection since if 'God' is a generic term then it must be the highest generic term in an ordered system, yet the 'highest' generic

45

terms ('unity' and 'being'), do *not* indicate genera as Aquinas, following Aristotle, makes clear (*Summa Theologica* Ia, q3, a5). Further, God is said to be the principle of all being, which rules 'God' out from being a generic term. On this account, God, as the principle of all being would be that in virtue of which 'exists', which has as many different senses as there are categories, can nevertheless be said to be non-homonymous. Hence, God cannot fall under any category, not even 'Substance', as Aquinas points out; neither can it be said that 'God' itself introduces a category since on this line of thought 'God' is the unifying principle of all categories. We have here then a case for supporting objection (5) and we also have the basis of an argument for rejecting the objections raised against (1)–(3). Category introducing items cannot sensibly be prefixed by a number (cf. *Tractatus* 4. 1272), hence that which is the principle of all categories, being of yet a higher order, cannot itself be sensibly so prefixed, hence 'God' as so understood by St Thomas, cannot be regarded as a descriptive predicable term prefixable by a number. Further, in that 'God' is an even 'higher' term than a category introducing one (a 'Formal concept' in Wittgenstein's sense, ibid.), 'God' cannot be regarded as a descriptive predicable term in the sense of a 'matter' or 'mass' term, for descriptive predicable terms in this sense can sensibly be prefixed by 'the same' (e.g. 'the same gold' or 'the same water'), whereas no category introducing term can. To think such an item can be so sensibly precursed is to radically confuse a 'formal' concept with a 'proper' one (cf. Wittgenstein, ibid.).

Objection (6) relies on the assumption that since 'God' is not to be confused with 'god' and the latter is a descriptive predicable term prefixable by the indefinite article, etc., the former cannot be. I have pointed out earlier that the conclusion in this assumption does not follow from the premises. It might be claimed that 'God' could perfectly well be a descriptive predicable term and that those assertions to the effect that God is a supreme being, or even *the* supreme being, still hold true in an important sense, namely, that whatever satisfied such a description would be a supreme being and if there were only one such entity, the supreme being. (The assertion that God is being itself need not worry us since it is a nonsensical one.) The difficulty about such a claim is that it takes no cognisance of Aquinas' point that God is the principle of being and in that God is so spoken of, as I above argued, then 'God' cannot be a descriptive predicable term. It might be objected that the idea of a principle of all being is a misguided one since one cannot raise the question 'On account of what (or, 'In virtue of what') are we able to have different but non-homonymous senses of 'exist' according to whether we are speaking of something which falls under the category of substance, quantity, quality etc?' (cf. *Metaphysics* 1017 a23–31). Any such charge of misguidedness would, I think, be based on one of the following claims: (a) that 'exists' does not have a different, though related, sense for different categories; 'exists' is univocal in sense (Quine);[11] (b) that 'exists' is irredeemibly homonymous (the early Aristotle subscribed to this view in the *Eudemian Ethics* as a backlash to Plato); (c) that, following a suggestion of the later Wittgenstein, the nature of human discourse is such that we can only seek for resemblances (and differences) between the various occurrences of 'exists' and not for any single unifying principle (or, for that matter, any single principle of differentiation). Such claims would have to be most thoroughly scrutinised before any such charge of inappropriateness could be upheld but this is not the place to pursue the matter. I draw the reader's attention to these points lest anyone should think that one can pretty easily reject the idea of a principle of all being in the sense explained.

Objection (7) presents us with the most serious difficulty so far. If it is the case that 'God' is a descriptive predicable term then the proposition 'God exists' is a possible one. Any general term which is not an inherently self-contradictory one (like 'round square') or a pretence one (like 'darlek') must be able to apply to something or other; and for it to have application to something or other is what it is for what is indicated by the general term to exist. As we have seen earlier, 'existence' in the sense with which we are now concerned is a predicate of a propositional function and derivatively of a class and it is of the nature of such general terms that they can occur in such functions. Does the doctrine 'God does not exist; He is eternal' commit us to the view that the proposition 'God exists'; $(\exists x)Gx$' is an impossible one? Only if (a) the sense of 'exist' in 'God does not exist; He is eternal' is that sense of 'exist' expressed by the quantifier or (b) if the sense of 'exists' expressed

47

by the quantifier presupposes that sense of exist expressed in 'God does not exist; He is eternal', if this is indeed a different sense to that so expressed.

The point of saying that 'God does not exist, He is eternal', is to draw our attention to the truth that God is not a spatio-temporal object. Whatever is God cannot be spoken of as coming into existence, going on existing, existing for a time and then ceasing to exist, occupying such and such a position in space or time, etc., whereas whatever is a man or a flower (e.g.) can be so spoken of. The sense of existence expressed here when it is said that God does not exist is that sense clearly set forth by Professor Geach in 'Form and Existence'[12] which he claims in Aquinas' sense of *esse*. Geach rightly distinguishes between this sense of 'exists' and that expressed by the quantifier in the proposition 'There is no such thing as a dragon; dragons do not exist'. On the use of 'exists' here pertinent (Geach's sense 'C') he comments:

> We have a sense of 'is' or 'exists' that seems to me to be certainly a genuine predicate of individuals: the sense of 'exists' in which we say that an individual came to exist, still exists, no longer exists.

This sense of 'exists' was also well noted by Aristotle: it is that sense of 'exists' introduced by his doctrine of τὸ ὂν καθ' αὑτό. To be in this sense is to be something or other, viz. to fall under some predicate falling under one of his 'categories'.[13] For Socrates to be is for Socrates to be a man, to have the kind of life that a man has; for the law against smoking in certain places to be is for the law to be in operation, i.e. enforceable; for the icicle over my back door to be is for there to be a certain lump of frozen water. Owen comments:

> English has an idiom which helps us to mark off such existential dicta from others . . . it lets us replace them with the predicate 'in existence'. In any language they have other marks; the predicate can be qualified by some adverbs of time 'still'; 'always', 'no longer' . . . and in different contexts we call on different predicates to contradict it – 'extinct': 'dead'; 'dismantled': 'disused'.[14]

The quantifier sense of 'exists' however (a) cannot apply to individuals for the quantifier asserts that there is an individual such that . . . (b) cannot be precursed by such epithets as 'still'; 'always'; 'no longer', viz. by such adverbs of time, so a clear distinction must be drawn between these two senses of 'exists'. Neither is it the case that either (a) the existential quantifier sense of 'exist' presupposes this presently discussed use or (b) is reducible to it. For to say that an individual *is*, in the sense under discussion, viz. that an individual is a ―― (where the blank takes some predicate), presupposes that there are $(\exists x)Fx$, men, laws, icicles, etc., for being in this sense to apply to and as this existential sense of 'is' is presupposed then it cannot presuppose the sense of 'is' under discussion or be reducible to it. Thus it does not follow from the fact that the sense of 'is' under discussion is totally inapplicable to God, that God cannot be said either to exist or fail to exist, viz. that 'God exists' $(\exists x)Gx$ is impossible.

There are, however, other grounds for holding that the proposition is an impossible one and that therefore 'God' cannot be regarded as an ordinary general term. What would make such a proposition an impossible one would be the impossibility of God having instantiation, or, to put it in more formal terms the impossibility of the term 'God' having application. Now it can be argued that this is indeed the case on the following grounds. The only individuals to which the predicable '―― is God' could truly or falsely apply would be individuals such that those individuals could not be said to be '*in* existence', viz. eternal, immutable, immortal, incorporeal individuals. But, it will be pressed, there can be no such class of things as the class of eternal, immutable, immortal, incorporeal individuals and hence no such individuals *per se*, since to say that X is eternal, immutable, immortal, incorporeal, is *not* to say what X *is*, or to say that X is a something or other, but to make a grammatical remark concerning X, to comment on the *character* of X, viz. to say that X can be spoken of in such and such ways as opposed to other ways. For example, to say that Love is eternal is to say that one cannot raise the questions 'When did Love come into existence?'; 'Does Love still exist?'; 'When will Love cease to exist?'. That is, to say that Love is eternal is to allocate it to a category, not a class. To this it might be replied as follows: 'Agreed, to say "X is eternal", etc., is not to say what X is, but even so there are three classes of things which can fall under this category which would be

49

relevant here, individuals falling under which classes could meaningfully be said to be God, viz. spirits, souls, intellectual creatures (cf. *Summa Theologica* Ia, q50, a1).' That 'spirit' cannot introduce a class of things, in this context cannot tell you *what* something is, has already been argued earlier; that 'soul' cannot perform this role has already been adequately argued by Geach in his paper 'Immortality'.[15] A soul is necessarily the soul of something or other and its identity is determined by and is logically dependent on that of which it is the soul. We distinguish between souls by distinguishing between that which is said to have the soul (e.g. in the case of human souls, the individual men). 'Soul' is thus a dependent concept and cannot supply us with an answer to the question of what something is; we have to know the answer to *this* question in order to know whether and in what sense we can 'attribute' a soul to the individual concerned. 'Intellectual creatures.' Aquinas (*Summa Theologica* Ia, q50, a1) raises the question of whether there is an entirely spiritual creature, altogether incorporeal, and argues that there must be some incorporeal creatures, for the perfection of the universe requires that there should be intellectual creatures which are 'pure intelligences'. However, an 'intelligence' if it can be said to be an existent at all, cannot be said to be an *independent* type of existent, for whilst, as Aquinas rightly argues, intelligence cannot be an operation or function of the body or a function of any faculty which the body has, it does not follow that intelligence is something that can have existence independent of a body of a certain kind. To have such an independent existence would entail that one could produce a criterion for the identity of individual intelligences which was totally independent of any criterion of identity for material bodies of a certain kind. Just this, however, is impossible because: (a) intelligence is necessarily the intelligence of someone or other or, possibly, if we allow that machines or animals may exhibit intelligence, of some thing or other; and (b) we determine the identity of an individual intelligence by reference to the identity of the man, animal, or machine of whom or of which it is the intelligence. For example, that you and I are both now talking about one and the same (individual) intelligence is only determinable by whether you and I are talking about one and the same man, or one and the same animal or machine who or which exhibits that intelligence. In

50

other words, the identity of individual intelligences is determined and only determinable by the identity of the men, etc., which exhibit that intelligence, as the identity of the individual soul is determined by and only determinable by the identity of the man or animal which 'has' the soul, which is to say that identity of men, animals, etc., is presupposed by identity of intelligence. Thus, 'incorporeal substances' such as intelligences or souls, cannot have independent identity and hence cannot have independent or separate existence. Thus there cannot be, to use Aquinas' phrase, 'altogether incorporeal substances'; in so far as there can be such 'incorporeal substances', they depend for their existence upon corporeal ones.

If the above argument is correct then 'God exists' '$(\exists x)Gx$' is an impossible proposition, for the only type of individual which could constitute an instance of being God are either (a) those which upon investigation turn out to be no individuals at all (e.g. 'spirit'; 'person'); or (b) dependent ones (e.g. 'soul'; 'intelligence'), yet it cannot be claimed that any individual which is such that the predicable '—— is God' might truly apply to it, is an individual which depends for its identity and existence upon the identity and existence of some other individual. Further, it can rightly be argued that (b) above introduces no class of individuals since for souls to exist is for creatures to exhibit a certain form of life. As Aristotle held, the soul is the *form* of the living body, but the *form* of the living body is not itself an entity but rather determines what an entity is.[16] Again, for intellectual creatures or intelligences to exist is for creatures of certain kinds to exhibit intelligence.

Professor Geach, who explicitly affirms in several places that 'God' is a 'descriptive predicable' term,[17] noticeably avoids the issue of what it is that the term 'God' can be affirmatively predicable. He says:[18]

> 'God exists' is true, if and only if, *the term* 'God' is affirmatively predicable. And what *this* is to say is that to say that there is a God is *true*, not because some divine attribute signified by 'There is' belongs to God, but because the divine attributes belong to something or other, just as blindness exists in that 'blind' is truly predicable of some eyes, not because blindness has the attribute of existing.[19]

The problem is: 'What is it which is such that the divine

51

attributes can apply to it?'; Geach has no difficulty in saying what blindness is truly predicable of, but then leaves the crucial question in the 'God' case unanswered.

It might be maintained that the crucial premise earlier invoked, viz. that the only individuals to which the predicable '—— is God' could truly or falsely apply, are eternal, immutable, incorporeal ones, is itself false. Let us assume for the moment that it is false and raise the question of whether the proposition 'God exists' is possible on the assumption that the type of individuals which can be said to be God are 'in time'. On such an assumption the proposition is equally impossible; God could never be instantiated, 'God' could never be satisfied, have application. On this assumption and any account based on this assumption, the type of individual in question is such that it can be said to 'come into existence', 'go on existing', 'still exist', 'cease to exist'. To say that it were possible for some individual or other of such a type to be God, would be to say that it is possible for an entity which exists in time and through a given period of time and can sensibly be spoken of as 'coming into existence', etc., to be eternal, i.e. not existing in time; immortal, i.e. cannot be spoken of as ceasing to exist; immutable, i.e. cannot be spoken of as changing, let alone going out of existence. In short, those predicates which indicate the 'nature' of God – 'eternal', 'immortal', 'immutable', etc., are such that they cannot truly or falsely apply to individuals of the type under consideration here; such a concept of individual rules out anything falling under that concept from being eternal, immortal, ummutable, etc.

An attempt may be made to answer this difficulty on the following lines, but it does not prove successful. It may be said that although it is of the nature of God to be eternal, immortal, immutable, etc., nevertheless it is possible for some individual of the type introduced here to be God. For, whilst it is indeed the case that being an individual in this sense necessarily implies being at least a temporal existent, it is *not* the case that for some individual to be God entails that that individual be eternal, immortal, immutable, etc. These attributes (and the corresponding predicates) are attributes (or predicates) of God, i.e. of the *nature* and it does not follow that they must also be attributes or predicates of that which is said to have the nature; indeed it would be a gross fallacy to so think. This line of

52

attack however will not do, since it is false that the 'Divine attributes' under discussion here are attributes *of* the nature, or the corresponding predicates predicates *of* the nature, or simply attributes or predicates of God. Such attributes constitute *part of God's essence*, i.e. constitute *part of his nature*. Such predicates constitute *part of the expression of that nature*. Again, the line of thought here advocated assumes that natures are something which individuals might have or possess, viz. something which is an accident of individuals. On the contrary, *for an individual to have a certain nature, is for an individual to be of that nature*. For Socrates to have the nature 'man', is not for Socrates 'to have something attached to him', but *to be* a man. In so far as (e.g.) Socrates is a man, whatever constitutes the nature of man, under some conception of 'man', holds true of Socrates the individual. Thus, if any individual is possibly to be said to be God, it must be possible for that individual to take on that which is the nature of God, which is impossible if the individuals concerned are in time.

I thus claim that here we have a strong case against the view that 'God' is an ordinary general term, for any such general term, as I argued at the beginning of this discussion, must be capable of applying to something or other, but there are no individuals which are such that the term 'God' could apply to them.

It might be said that if this contention is correct then such propositions as 'Jesus Christ is God' and 'The Holy Spirit is God' are impossible. This does not so follow; all that follows is that such sentences as 'Jesus Christ is God' and 'The Holy Spirit is God' cannot be construed as expressing propositions parallel to (e.g.) 'Socrates is a man' or 'Joseph is a man', i.e. propositions of an ordinary subject–predicate kind.

(8) It will be objected that this is a thoroughly misguided piece of reasoning as a whole, since in the subject–predicate proposition 'Socrates is a man', we cannot treat '(a) man' as the predicate. The predicate is '—— is (a) man'. Hence we cannot perform the operation which leads to the equally objectionable proposition 'A man socratises'. This latter proposition is objectionable since it assumes that a proper name *can* genuinely occur as a predicate, which it cannot do. It treats a proper name as a 'mini-predicate', when a proper name is no predicate at all; hence the patent artificiality of the form 'socratises'.[20]

Even accepting this objection however we might still think that there is a point to be made here – namely, that in the case of an ordinary general term occurring as a putative subject, this is exponible, not as a single word, but as a word preceded by the indefinite article. Such a case cannot be made out; 'Gold' is such a term, yet when it occurs as a putative subject term as in 'Gold was desired by the misers of old', we cannot preface it by the indefinite article. On these grounds (8) above presents us with no genuine objection.

(9) by contrast this objection does. Professor Geach has recently presented us with the most illuminating account of Aquinas' doctrine of Form and I shall now turn to that account as a basis for discussion here. According to Geach:[21]

> . . . the expression for a form is either a logical predicate like '—— is red', or in the subject position, an expression requiring completion with the name of an individual – 'The redness of ——' or, equivalently 'that by which —— is red' . . . The last two types of expression (the second of them especially common in Aquinas) are reminiscent of functional signs in mathematics like 'log' or 'sin' which are completable by numerical signs.

Geach has had more to say on this earlier.[22] It transpires from this discussion that according to his account, what Aquinas intends by 'Form' can be paralleled to what is meant by function in mathematics. A 'Form' is what is signified by an expression of the form 'The —— of/ ——' (e.g. 'The square root of /——' or ' —— is red'). Such a Form as 'The square root of /——' Geach later calls Forms *tout court* to differentiate them from individualised Forms (e.g. 'The Wisdom of Socrates').[23] What is important to note here, according to Geach, is that *the whole phrase* expressing an individualised Form cannot be analysed. 'The wisdom of Socrates' is not such that one can construe the phrase as 'The wisdom that belongs to Socrates' and *then* ask what sort of entity 'Wisdom' is and what sort of relation is signified by 'belongs to'.[24] The whole phrase 'The wisdom of Socrates' or 'The square root of 4' must, on the contrary, be construed as 'The wisdom of/Socrates': 'The square root of/4'. On this account of Form, for God to be a Form, is for 'God' to be writable as ' —— is God', and hence it must in principle be possible to supply an 'argument', viz. an

54

individual value for the blank here which has the role of an 'argument place'. But just this would demand what Aquinas denies, viz. that the Form *God* is individualised by being received in a subject as the Form '—— is wise' or 'The wisdom of ——' *is* individualised by being received in a subject, i.e. is individualised in that we supply a value for the blank in the function 'The wisdom of ——', thus yielding the expression for the individualised Form 'the wisdom of Socrates'. Contrary to 'ordinary' Forms, God is not individuated by being 'received in matter' or by 'being received by many' as 'ordinary' Forms, such as what is signified by '—— is (a) man' or '—— is red' are, but is individuated 'precisely because it cannot be received in a subject'.[25] Yet any general term (save a self-contradictory or deliberately fictional one) *is* such that it can be 'received in a subject', i.e. is instantiable, as I argued earlier; it is such that it can 'be received by many', viz. have application to many individuals, be satisfied by many individuals.

Further, on Geach's account of 'Form', when an expression for a Form stands in the subject position, it is of the form 'The F of ——', where the blank is filled out by the name of an individual or the names of individuals. If 'God' is thus the expression for a Form in the ordinary sense, then 'God' as occurring in the subject position is *always* writable as 'The God of ——' and so we should have as an example of an individualised Form 'The God of Abraham' or 'The God of Isaac'. Now not only does this go against Aquinas' doctrine that God is not a Form which is individualised by being received in a subject, but also one can see why it is impossible that the Form *God* should be so individualised. To make the Form so individualised would be to make it the case that it is necessarily the case that God is the God of someone or other or something or other, as the square root is necessarily the square root of some (rational) number, or redness is necessarily the redness of some object. And it is just this contention which will be denied, for it is neither the case that: (a) God's identity is logically dependent on the identity of something else, nor that (b) God's existence is logically dependent upon the existence of something else.

In the case of either 'The square root of 4' or 'The wisdom of Socrates', we can only identify the square root concerned by reference to the number of which it is the square root; we can

55

only identify the particular wisdom by reference to the particular man whose wisdom it is. But it cannot be maintained that we can only identify God by reference to the individuals whose names can be substituted for the blank in the phrase 'The God of ——' such that a true proposition is yielded when we have the complete sentence (e.g.) 'The God of Abraham told Abraham to sacrifice his son Isaac', for it is not necessary that God is the God *of* Abraham, Isaac, Jacob, etc., or the God *of* Israel. God does not gain 'His' identity by reference to such individuals or such a group. This can be seen by the fact that 'God' is introduced into the scriptures without reference to such individuals; it would not be possible to understand such passages as:

> Now the Lord said unto Abram, Get thee out of thy country and from thy kindred (Genesis 12.1);
> And the Lord said unto Abram, after Lot was separated from him, Lift up now thine eyes and look from the place where thou art, northward and southward eastward and westward, for all the land which thou seest to thee will I give it and to thy seed for ever (Genesis 12.14, 15);
> And when Abram was ninety years old and nine, the Lord appeared unto Abram and said unto him; I am God Almighty, walk before me and be thou perfect (Genesis 17.1);

if it were necessarily the case that God were (e.g.) the God of Abraham.

In the case of either 'The square root of 4' or 'The Wisdom of Socrates' the existence of such a square root or such a wisdom is dependent on the prior existence of the number four and Socrates respectively. If there were no such thing as the number four or Socrates then there could be no such thing as the square root of 4 or the wisdom of Socrates. But it cannot be the case that God's existence is so logically dependent on the existence of something else, for He is said to be the Creator of all things (save the persons of the Trinity) and hence cannot be dependent on them for His existence.

(10) This is also a serious difficulty for the thesis that 'God' is an ordinary general term and if the thesis that 'God' is an abstract term can be maintained such a thesis explains some puzzling features of Christian Theology:

56

(i) Aquinas' point that God is not a Form which can be received in matter or 'received by many', since, if anything can be said to be designated by an abstract term then whatever is so designated cannot either be (a) received in matter, or (b) received by many. Take Love and Wisdom as examples. If it is asserted that Socrates is loving or wise, or that Plato is loving or wise, then we cannot say that here we have two instances of the Form 'Love' (with a capital 'L') or 'Wisdom' (with a capital 'W') either being 'received in matter' or 'received by many', for to so say would entail that that which was eternal, immutable, a-spatial (viz. the Form 'Love' or 'Wisdom') was also temporal, mutable and spatial. In other words it would commit one to saying that that which was transcendent was also immanent. It is worth commenting that Parmenides, in Plato's dialogue of that name, insists that there can be no relation between the Forms and particulars for this reason (amongst others).[26]

(ii) The feature above discussed, namely that God is necessarily not the God of any particular or of any group of particulars; as the hymn says: 'Thou art simply *God*'.

(iii) That feature of Christian Theology which maintains, not simply that (e.g.) God is good or wise or even infinitely good or infinitely wise but that either: (a) God is His own goodness or wisdom, or (b) God *is* Goodness or Wisdom. Certainly in at least the latter case, the only possible position to maintain is that 'God' *is* an abstract term and to say that God is Goodness, Wisdom, or Love must be to maintain that God is identical with the designation of these abstract terms. As 'Logician' has commented in Professor Prior's paper 'Can religion be discussed?':

The alternatives I had in mind were proper or common (nouns) on the one hand, and *abstract* on the other. On the face of it, as you say, 'God' looks like a common or proper noun. Qualities are predicated of Him – 'God is good'; and in the sentence we are considering, you speak of 'His own goodness'. But then you say that God *is* this 'goodness'; that is, he is not a thing or person at all, but an abstraction.[27]

Now it might be pressed that whilst there is indeed a case for saying that in so far as (b) above holds, then 'God' is an abstract term. Nevertheless, we can certainly offer an account of

57

(a) above, without supposing that 'God' is such a term. Indeed Professor Geach has attempted such an account and this must now be examined. On the contention that God is his own wisdom, Geach writes:

> . . . we *can* take it to mean that 'God' and 'the wisdom of God' are two names of the same thing . . . For we can significantly say that 'God' and 'the wisdom of God' and 'the power of God' are three names with the same reference, but 'the wisdom of . . .'; 'the power of . . .' have not the same reference any more than the predicates 'wise' and 'powerful' have.[28]

Thus, on this account, to say that God is the same as his nature, is to make a remark concerning the reference of certain names. Geach cites a mathematical example as an analogy for the 'God' case – the example being 'the square root of 25'. In this case 'the square root of 25' and '5' designate the same number, namely the number 5. A similar case is developed for 'the square of 1' 'the cube of 1' and '1'. 'The square' and 'the cube' are quite distinct functions but '1', 'the square of 1' and 'the cube of 1' all designate the same number – 1.

My objections to Geach's analogy are as follows:

(i) It is sensible (and Geach here is only concerned with sense) to talk of 'the square of 1', 'the cube of 1' and '1' as having the *same* reference or designation since we can specify *what* the reference or designation of these items is; in each case it is the number 1. Unless we can say *what* the reference or designation of 'The wisdom of God', 'the power of God', and 'God' is, we cannot sensibly speak of these three 'names' having the same reference or designation. Geach offers us no parallel to 'the number 1' in the God case, but it seems clear from his general line of thought that the parallel he would offer is 'The same god' – such that the three names designate one and the same god and that we can provide a uniquely identifying description in relation to such a god. But the provision of such a formulation radically confuses 'god' and 'God'; a confusion I have been keen to entangle earlier. The fundamental difficulty here is that we cannot, *contra* the mathematical case, specify what the reference is, for any putative specification fails and to attempt such a specification would immediately contra-

58

dict the classical point that God is not in any genus. Further, the notion of 'reference' here is peculiar (to say the least), for the notion of 'reference' has its home and place in a spatial scheme, yet God is not 'in' any such scheme, and is unlike numbers in that 'His' identity does not presuppose an implicit reference to the idea of space.[29]

(ii) If the use of the name 'God' is to be paralleled to the use of the name 'I' (and the use of the name 'Socrates'), then 'God' becomes like 'I' or 'Socrates' a *nomen individuiis*, which is certainly denied by Aquinas and in other places most emphatically by Geach himself. If we are to take as parallels 'The square of ——' and 'The wisdom of ——', then what can stand in the argument place of these functions are individual constants, whereas for Geach 'God' is precisely not such a constant.

Geach himself tackles this problem. He says:

> If 'God' is a predicative expression, how can it significantly stand in the place of a proper name like 'Socrates', after 'the wisdom of' or 'the power of'? I think it enough to reply that 'God' in *such* contexts or indeed in subject position before 'is wise' or 'is powerful' has the force of a definite description 'the one and only God'; whatever our theory of descriptions may be it will have to yield the result that a definite description can significantly take the place of a proper name, as a subject of a proposition or again after a phrase like 'the wisdom of'.[30]

This reply clearly relies on the position that a definite description can stand as a subject of a proposition and is not to be taken as Russell takes it. Even granted this, for reasons offered earlier, an additional argument has to be produced to show that a definite description can significantly take the place of a proper name after a phrase like 'the wisdom of'. Further, even if such an argument is produced, the following problem still remains: *Granted* that in such contexts, as Geach mentions, 'God' is writable as 'The one and only God', *which* proper name is it that 'God', as so construed, takes the place of?' Geach makes no suggestions here; we might suggest 'Almighty' as the appropriate name, or 'Holy', following Aquinas' point at *Summa Theologica* Ia, q13, a1, but if we do then it is quite unclear how we can offer an account of what it is to say that God is his essence or nature following Geach's account.

(iii) How is it decidable that the 'three names' – 'The Wisdom of God', 'The power of God' and 'God' – have the same reference or designation? In the mathematical case it is decidable that '$\sqrt{25}$' and '5' have the same designation in virtue of the very rules for the use of such items. Professor Geach offers us no account in the 'God' case.

(iv) It is not clear how such items as 'The power of God' or 'The wisdom of God' can be taken as names. On Geach's own account they are expressions of individualised Forms; but from this it does not follow that they are names or can be taken as names. Indeed it seems impossible that they should be taken as names for on Geach's own account such items are analogous to mathematical functions, yet such functions are not names; $\sqrt{25}$ is 5, $\sqrt{25}$ does not name 5. Such items as 'The wisdom of Socrates', even if they can be said to refer, are not names. 'The wisdom of Socrates' does not name anything which Socrates possesses; yet this is what Professor Geach seems to require for his account to be adequate.

It is only fair to comment that Geach has revised his position somewhat in the version of his paper which appears in *God and the Soul*. At the appropriate place he writes:

> When Aquinas tells us that God is wisdom itself, *Deus est ipsa sapienta*, he is not meaning that God is that of which the noun 'wisdom' is a proper name; for the Platonists are wrong in thinking that there is such an object, and Aquinas says that they are wrong. But we *can* take it to mean that 'God' and 'the wisdom of God' both designate the same thing; and this interpretation does not make Aquinas guilty of the impossible and nonsensical attempt to bridge the distinction previously expounded between form and individual, or find something intermediate. For we can significantly say that 'God' and 'the wisdom of God' and 'the power of God' are three terms with the same reference; but 'the wisdom of . . .' and 'the power of . . .' have not the same reference, any more than the predicates 'wise' and 'powerful' have. (p. 51)

On this account 'God' and 'the wisdom of God' are not asserted to be names, but they are nevertheless said to designate the same thing and hence the problem raised in my objection (i) is still pertinent. Further, even though my objection (ii) is technically, at first sight, no objection to the revised version, in

60

so far as Geach still does want to draw the analogy with the mathematical examples, the point of this objection still holds (cf. p. 52). Likewise, although 'the wisdom of God', etc., are no longer said to be names, in so far as Geach implies that we can speak of the same designation in these cases, my objection (iii) is pertinent (cf. p. 52). On the revised version it is only my objection (iv) which ceases to carry any weight, for Geach does seem to have withdrawn the contention that such phrases as 'the power of God', etc., are *names*, even though they designate. How far objection (iv) can be genuinely withdrawn, however, as opposed to being withdrawn on a technicality, is a matter of doubt since in his 'Preface' to *God and the Soul*, he describes the relevant changes as 'stylistic'.

Can any other account of the thesis that God is his own goodness or wisdom be offered and does such an account commit one to the view that 'God' is an abstract term? The most profitable thing to do here is to turn to Aquinas' own argument for the contention that God is his nature:

> *I answer that* God is the same as his essence or nature. To understand this, it must be noted that in things composed of matter and form the nature or essence (*natura: essentia*) must differ from the *suppositum*, because the essence or nature includes (*comprehendit*) only what defines the species of a thing: thus human nature (humanity) *humanitas* includes only what defines man, or what makes man man. . . . Now individual matter, with all the individual accidents is not included in the definition of the species. . . . Therefore this flesh, these bones and the accidental qualities distinguishing this particular matter are not included in human nature (humanity) and yet they are included in the thing which is a man. Hence the thing which is a man has something more to it than has humanity. Consequently humanity (human nature) and a man are not wholly identical. 'Humanity' (human nature) signifies the formative element in man . . . On the other hand in things not composed of matter and form, in which individualisation is not due to individual matter – that is to say, to *this* matter, the very forms being individualised of themselves – it is necessary that the forms themselves should be subsisting *supposita*. Therefore suppositum and nature in them

61

are identified. Since God then is not composed of matter and form, He must be His own Godhead, His own life, and whatever else is thus predicated of Him (*Summa Theologica* Ia, q3, a3).

As the thesis that God is His own nature is reached via a complex philosophical argument, to understand what is being put forward it is necessary to understand the stages in that argument; to accept the thesis entails accepting the positions advocated in the premises of the argument and accepting the argument as valid.

A.   What are things composed of matter and form? From Aquinas' own examples here and from one tradition which he is following (the Aristotelian one), we can instance at least animals, men, viz. countable entities in the sense of entities which fall under a term which can furnish a unit of counting in its own right; 'man' and 'animal' furnish us with just such terms.[31]

B.   What is the distinction between matter and form and what is it to say that things which are so composed, *are* so composed? Two accounts can, I think, be offered:

(I) For any individual A, which is such that it falls under a type F, where 'F' is a predicate which can furnish a unit of counting in its own right, then we must distinguish formally between: (a) that in virtue of which A is F (the 'Form' of A) – call it F' – and (b) A itself, viz. the individual which has the Form in virtue of which A is F. This distinction is necessary since in regard to the 'Form' there is a set of formal predicates which are such that they rule out any Form being an individual and in regard to 'individual' there is a set of formal predicates which rule out any individual from being a Form. In the case of the Form such predicates are 'being instantiable'; 'being present in'. In the case of the individual such predicates are 'being an instance of'; 'having the possibility of spatio-temporal location or of either spatial or temporal location'; 'being individuated by reference to a certain matter and the accidents of such matter'. These sets of formal predicates are mutually exclusive. Nothing can both (e.g.) be instantiable *and* be an instance of, be individuated by reference to a certain matter and fail to be so individuated. Yet having made such a distinction we must assert a 'composition' since we must be able to say in virtue of

62

what any individual f is an F. The answer to this lies in the Form. On this account, then, to say that A (an individual) is 'composed of' matter is simply to say that A is of matter, i.e. can be identified by reference to some material principle (e.g. A is a lump of gold; A is a piece of silver; A is a mass of flesh and bone). To say that A is 'composed of' Form is simply to say that A (an identified lump of matter) falls under some Form F' in virtue of which A is F.

(II) For any individual A which is such that it falls under a type F, where 'F' is a predicate which can supply us with a unit of counting, then we must distinguish formally between (a) the concept F (the Form F) introduced by the predicate F, and (b) the individual A (which is Y where 'Y' introduces a term which can form a criterion of continued identity), which instances that concept F.

This is necessary since in regard to such concepts as introduced by predicates which can furnish us with units of counting (such as 'man'; 'animal'), there is a set of formal predicates (such as 'being instantiable'; 'having the possibility of application') which apply to the concept in question but which cannot sensibly apply to the individual x which instances that concept, to which the predicate introducing the concept has application. Conversely, there is a set of formal predicates which apply to the individual x to which such predicates apply, which cannot be sensibly applied to the concepts introduced by such predicates themselves – e.g. 'being an instance of'; 'that to which a predicate introducing a concept (of the type in question) applies'; 'being individuated by reference to a certain matter and the accidents of such matter'; 'being identified by reference to some criterion of continued identity which is a material principle'. On this account to say that some individual, say A, is 'composed of' matter is simply to say that A is of matter, i.e. can be identified by reference to some material principle (e.g. 'A is a lump of gold, a piece of silver, a chunk of flesh and bones'). To say that A is 'composed of' Form is simply to say that A, an identified and individualised piece of matter falls under some Form of the type introduced, i.e. is an instance of some Form of the type introduced such that the propositional function 'x is F' is true for that value of x which is A.

The difference between these two accounts is clear enough but important. Both accounts take 'Things composed of matter and

63

Form' as referring to individuals falling under some concept introduced by a term which furnishes a unit of counting in its own right, but (I) construes the Form of A as that in virtue of which the individual A is F (e.g. that in virtue of which an identified and individualised piece of matter is able to be said to be a man or a horse); whilst (II) construes the Form of A as what is introduced by F itself. Hence, according to account (I) 'man', 'horse', 'animal', i.e. terms which can introduce units of counting in their own right, do not *themselves* introduce Forms, but introduce that which may be said to *have* a Form and individuals which fall under such concepts do so fall by virtue of having this Form: whereas according to account (II) 'man', 'horse', 'animal' (e.g.) *do* themselves introduce Forms. This confusion in the concept of 'Form', I suspect goes right back to Aristotle, for in some passages Aristotle speaks of 'Form' as what answers his 'τί ἐστι' question when asked of an individual already identified by reference to some material principle, which answer *would* yield us with such terms as 'man', 'horse' etc.,[32] whereas in other places he speaks of the Form as (a) that of which the verbal expression is a definition[33] and hence something which (e.g.) man or horse *has* or *possesses*; (b) something by virtue of which something which is already identified by reference to some material principle *is what it is*. As Professor Anscombe has put it:

> The form then is what makes what a thing is made *of* into that thing. It may be literally a shape, as it is the shape that makes bronze into a statue or again an arrangement (e.g.) of letters to make a syllable; or a position, as the position of a beam makes a threshold or lintel, or a time as the time of eating food makes that food breakfast.[34]

Granted these two accounts one must now ask which account reflects Aquinas' thought. To attribute the first account to him would entail saying that Form = Essence (*essentia*) or nature, which would (a) be natural in the light of the opening section of the passage cited above and would further be natural if we consider the following later passage in relation to the opening passage:

> ... but humanity is taken to mean the formal part of a man because the principles whereby a thing is defined are regarded

64

as the formal constituent in regard to the individualising matter.

(b) cohere with Aristotle's view that the Form of X *is* the essence (τὸ τί ἦν εἶναι) or nature of X[35], though it is of the greatest importance to note that Aristotle's 'τὸ τί ἦν εἶναι' is distinctly not expressed or expressible by an abstract term as Aquinas' Form here is; (c) be consistent with one account of 'Form' offered by Geach, i.e. that account in terms of 'that by which' "—— is red"', but, importantly, would not be consistent with his emphasised account of what Aquinas so means (cf. below).

On the second account one can offer no account of 'Things *not* composed of matter and form', for on this account 'Form' is not itself the nature of a composite, but rather the expression of the Form is the specification of a composite, for on this account to say that A is 'composed of' Form is to say that A, an identified and individualised piece of matter, falls under some Form of the type introduced by 'man' or 'animal'. On this account we can give no sense to 'Things not composed of matter and Form' for to give sense would be tantamount to saying that there could be concepts of the type in question which could have nothing falling under them, viz. were necessarily non-instantiable; whereas it is necessary that any such concept should be such that it is instantiable. Now according to Geach, Aquinas' 'Form' can be regarded as Frege's 'Concept', which would commit him to the second interpretation, for Frege's 'Concepts', paradigmatically, are introduced by such terms as can supply us with units of counting in their own right (e.g. 'man', 'horse') and which are necessarily instantiable. Hence, on Geach's rendering of 'Form' it does not seem possible to offer an account of 'Things not composed of matter and Form', i.e. 'Things "composed of" Form' only.

In the light of these considerations I shall take the first account (I) as reflecting Aquinas' thought. What must be noted on this account is that the Form by virtue of which the individual A is F is an abstraction – 'human nature' or 'humanity'. Thus it seems that in answer to the question 'By virtue of what is this individual mass of flesh and bones F (a man)?', we get 'By virtue of the Form "humanity" being present in this flesh and bones'. This closely reflects Plato's view that an individual A can be said to be large because it participates in the

Form 'The Large' (Largeness). But as has often been pointed out, saying that A participates in the Form 'F-ness' or 'The F' cannot answer the question 'By virtue of what is A an F?'. We cannot, for example, say that Socrates is a man by virtue of the Form 'Humanity' or 'Human nature' being present in Socrates, since for Socrates to be a man *is* for Socrates to be human. It is not necessary for our present purposes to investigate Plato's Theory of Forms; it is sufficient to note that on the account here being considered (I), the Form of what is introduced by 'F', where 'F' is a term which supplies us with a unit of counting in its own right, is an abstraction and the essence or nature of F is equally an abstraction.

To continue with the investigation of Aquinas' argument for the thesis that God is the same as his essence or nature. Aquinas maintains that in things composed of matter and Form (e.g. man), the nature or essence (*natura*; *essentia*) must differ from the *suppositum* because the essence or nature signifies only what is included in the definition of the species, viz. it is necessary to distinguish between what is referred to or denoted by such an abstract term as 'humanity' and what is referred to or denoted by what can stand as the subject of propositions, i.e. (paradigmatically) proper names, since the account of what is referred to by such an abstract term will contain only items which form part of a definition and not items which can form principles of individuation for particulars. This position commits Aquinas to maintaining that (a) one can ask 'What is signified by, i.e. understood by, the definition of a species?' to which the answer is in terms of an abstract term such as 'humanity'; (b) one can ask 'What is signified by, i.e. referred to or denoted by, the definition of a species?' to which the answer is the reference or denotation of such an abstract term, both of which answers are open to objection. One cannot raise the question (a) above since to furnish a definition is to answer the question 'What is understood by (signified by) X (where 'X' is a species)?'. Having obtained an answer one cannot *then* go on to ask the further question of what is understood by the definition, without committing a version of the fallacy of self-predication, namely, asking of the definition what one can only properly ask of the definiendum and concomitantly attributing to the definition predicates which one can only sensibly attribute to the definiendum. One can raise the question raised in (b) above, but as

66

Aristotle pointed out, it is misguided to think that there is *anything else*, viz. in the case of man, *humanity*, which is referred to or denoted by the definition. What is referred to or denoted by the definition of a species is at the least the sum of the individual members, at the most the species *man*. We might have reservations about saying that what is denoted by the definition is a kind or species on the grounds that for the kind or species to exist is for there to be individuals falling under that kind or species, but even if it is necessary to introduce kinds or species into our ontology on the grounds that there are some predicates which are asserted to hold true of the kind or species which do not hold true of the particulars, it is not necessary and indeed wrong to go any further than this; wrong, since no illumination whatsoever is gained by simply positing an abstraction and if we do so posit we are left with the further problem of what the relation is between the abstraction so posited and the definiendum.

To say that the individualising matter with all the individualising accidents is not included in the definition of the species is to say that the definition of (e.g.) man does not include as part of itself the description of individuals which fall under it. One must comment that one would not expect a definition *per genus et differentia* to so include; such a definition is not a list of the particular properties individuals satisfying that definition have. Yet, having made a distinction between (i) predicates which specify the uniquely distinguishing characteristics of an individual, and (ii) predicates which can only occur in a definition, Aquinas continues:

> . . . therefore this flesh, these bones, and the accidental qualities distinguishing this particular matter are not included in humanity; yet they are included in the thing which is a man. Hence the thing which is a man has something *more* in it than humanity.

In what sense of 'more' and why? The explanation of this would seem to be that since, as regards any individual piece of matter, we introduce both individuating predicates and a type of predicate such as 'humanity' introducing a Form which is signified by, i.e. denoted by, a definition, the introduction of individuating predicates constitutes an *addition*. Now it is only possible to speak of an *addition* here if *both* the individual and

67

the type introduced by (e.g.) 'humanity', viz. the Form, can take on the *same* type of predicates, which is only possible if one treats the Form itself as a type of individual, which, it might be argued was one of Plato's mistakes. But one is only led to construing the Form itself as a type of individual if one construes abstract terms as a species of name; whereas one cannot raise the question of the bearer or reference of an abstract term as one can in the case of genuine names. It is to be noted that if one had taken the second account of 'Form' as discussed above (II), then one would be forced to conclude that St Thomas radically confused 'concept' and 'object' (in Frege's sense), for on this account St Thomas would be saying that that which is a man has something more to it than *man* (Form) has, which would only be possible if both *man* and that which is a man can take on the same types of predicate, which in turn would commit him to treating an individual as in the same category as the reference of the type predicate 'man', viz. of conflating 'object' and 'concept'.

To turn to 'things not composed of matter and Form'. Here, to put the matter formally, we are dealing with a different type of term from those introduced earlier, i.e. 'man'; 'horse'. In this case, whilst we can still make the distinction between individual and concept, individual and predicate (F), the individual is not of the same type as that previously introduced, for in this case the identity of any individual is *not decidable* by reference to the *type* of individuating predicate previously introduced, viz. by reference to 'matter' terms and accidental material terms. In this type of case, for which Aquinas unfortunately gives us no examples, the identity of the individuals is the identity of the Form – as he has it 'the very Forms become individualised of themselves', viz. the Forms *themselves* become individuals – 'it is necessary that the Forms themselves should be subsisting *supposita*'. But, as I argued above, it is quite misguided to treat the Form itself as a type of individual, for on the first account of 'Form' offered above (I) this would be to treat an abstract term as itself the name of an individual. Aquinas concludes that in things not composed of matter and Form, of which God is a paradigm example, *suppositum* and nature are to be identified. This conclusion can only be arrived at by (a) treating a Form, i.e. the reference or denotation of an abstract term, as itself an individual; (b) taking as 'Things which are not composed of matter and Form' whatever is signified by an abstract term. Thus, in the 'God' case there is no distinction between the individual designated by 'God' and 'His' essence or nature, since God is the reference of the abstract term 'God', yet the reference of an abstract term is a nature, as we saw earlier.

3. In the light of these considerations there is a strong case for the view that 'God' is not to be regarded as an ordinary general term (Frege's 'concept term'), able to be prefixed by a number and occur in the formula '—— exists', where the blank takes a general term. Equally, however, there are cases in which 'God' does not exhibit these features, but does exhibit those features exhibited by ordinary substantival general terms. Since one cannot reduce the one to the other, one is forced to the conclusion that 'God' exhibits different and inconsistent logical properties, for a term cannot be both an abstract one and an ordinary general one let alone a particular type of general term (substantival). The difficulties which arise concerning the form of proposition sentences of the form 'God is F' can be said to express if we treat 'God' as an ordinary general term or as an abbreviation for a definite description, I have already introduced and discussed. The problem which now faces one is 'What form of proposition can be said to be expressed by sentences of the form 'God is F', where 'God' here is an abstract term?'

4. At this point it will be pressed that sentences of the form 'God is F', where 'God' is an abstract term, might be said to express propositions of a subject–predicate kind since whilst an argument has been produced for saying that if 'God' is a term of a substantival kind it cannot occur as a logical subject, no argument has been produced to show that 'God' as an abstract term cannot so occur and Professor Strawson has argued that 'anything whatever can appear as a logical subject, an individual. If we define "being an individual" as "being able to appear as an individual" then anything whatever is an individual'.[36]

Strawson's argument to this effect depends, in the first place, on his extension of the subject–predicate distinction to allow that universals may appear as logical subjects. It is my contention that this extension breaks down. On p. 171 of *Individuals* he argues:

> . . . to allow that universals may be predicated of universals we have to show that there are non-relational ties between universals and universals analogous to the characterising or sortal ties between universals and particulars. And of course it is easy to find such analogies.

In spite of claiming that it is easy to find such analogies his first example has to be put in the form of a question – 'Is not thinking of different species as species of one genus analogous to thinking of different particulars as specimens of one species?' This is put in the form of a question, I suggest, precisely because it is not clear in what way there is an important analogy between the two types of case such that important conclusions vis-à-vis a term being able to stand as a logical subject can be drawn. There is an analogy in that in both cases we have a case of something being subsumed under something, but this is as far as the analogy will go since the mode of being subsumed is importantly different in each case. In the first case we have an instance of the relation of class inclusion; in the second an instance of the relation of class membership. In order for an analogy of any consequence to be drawn between (a) the sortal or characterising ties between universals and particulars, and (b) the ties between (i) a species and a genus, or (ii) sub-types of musical form and their common form, one has to assume that either a species or a sub-type is itself, in some way, a generalised form of particular or that a particular is itself a mini-species or a mini-type. Such assumptions are however impossible for they would commit us to the view that there is no ultimate and absolute distinction between proper names and predicables; that there is has already been argued earlier. Strawson's further examples are also open to the same objection. Thinking of different hues or colours as bright or sombre, or thinking of different human qualities as aimiable or unaimiable, is only analogous to thinking of different particulars as characterised in such and such ways in any way which will involve important repercussions for the issue of what can stand as logical subjects if we regard types of hues or sub-species of colours or human qualities as themselves in some way types of particulars, which we could do only on the above impossible assumptions.

70

Further, in order for 'God' to have the possibility of appearing as a logical subject by analogy, viz. in the extended sense of 'logical subject' as introduced by Strawson, even *granting* his 'extended' sense, then 'God' must be regardable as a term which is a non-particular principle of collection, analogous to the way in which a predicate of particulars collects particulars (*vide* p. 226). But this requirement would demand that God was either a species or a genus or a sub-type in relation to a common form (see the examples cited from p. 171), which demand is impossible, for God is neither a species of a genus nor subsumable under any further common form. Thus, even if it can be argued that 'God' can meet Strawson's first requirement for occurring as a logical subject, viz. that God can be identifyingly introduced into a proposition (p. 226), it cannot meet the second, viz. it cannot be 'brought under some principle of collection of like things' and hence cannot appear as a logical subject. One might further comment, for the sake of completion, that God either proves the exception to Strawson's rule that nothing can be identifyingly introduced into a proposition without also being brought under some general principle of collection of like things or God is not 'anything whatever'. It seems to me that we must affirm the second alternative.

I commented above 'Thus even if it can be argued that "God" can meet Strawson's first requirement for occurring as a logical subject, viz. that God can be identifyingly introduced into a proposition . . .', but if 'God' is an abstract term, then it cannot perform such a function. 'Goodness', for example, in 'Goodness is what all men seek' or 'Beauty' in 'Beauty is in the eye of the beholder', cannot perform such a function, since no abstract term can perform a referring role and hence cannot perform the role of 'identifyingly referring' (in Strawson's sense) and the subsequent role of 'identifyingly introducing'. One cannot ask 'What is referred to by "Goodness" or "Beauty"?' precisely because Goodness and Beauty *are* abstractions.

5. What analysis of propositions expressed by sentences of the form 'God is F', where 'God' is an abstract term, are we to offer in the light of the difficulties raised in my last section? We might suggest that such sentences are to be taken as putting forward propositions of identity, but to do so we should have to reformulate such sentences in the form 'God is F' or, to cope with

71

sentences of the form 'God is infinitely F', 'God is infinite F', where 'F' takes as values the abstract noun form of the former adjective F (e.g. 'God is Wisdom'; 'God is Goodness' or 'God is infinite Wisdom'; 'God is infinite Goodness'). But even granted that such a reformulation is possible, sentences of the form 'God is infinite F' or 'God is F' cannot be said to express propositions of identity since there cannot be any such thing as (e.g.) Wisdom, which is not the wisdom of something or other;[37] equally there cannot simply be infinite wisdom but only the infinite wisdom of something or other or someone or other and hence we have not here an item in a possible identity relation. In general, as there cannot be F-ness which is not the F-ness of a,[38] likewise there cannot be infinite F-ness which is not the infinite F-ness of a. Yet if we introduce that of which the infinite F-ness is the infinite F-ness *of* in this case (or that of which the F-ness is the F-ness *of*), we no longer have an abstraction and hence no longer have the possibility of an identity relation holding between two abstract entities signified by two abstract terms. Further, in order to have a genuine proposition of identity here, even if we could get over the above difficulty, we must be prepared to say in what the identity consists and this we cannot do. For example, if we assert that Socrates and the husband of Xanthippe are identical then we are prepared, and must be prepared to expand as follows: 'Socrates' and 'The husband of Xanthippe' have the same reference, refer to the same man; again if we assert that $\sqrt{25}$ and 5 are identical then we are prepared, and must be prepared to expand as '$\sqrt{25}$' and '5' have the same reference, namely refer to the same number. But what can provide the parallel account necessary in the case under consideration? 'God is identical with infinite Goodness (Goodness)' – 'God' and 'infinite Goodness' refer to the same *what*? The only possible candidate seems to be 'the same existent (entity)' but this candidate is a non-starter since 'being' is not a genus. The inability to provide any completion for 'the same' here determines that such sentences as 'God is Goodness (infinite Goodness)' cannot be regarded as putting forward propositions of identity even if they can get as far as being regarded as putting forward a genuine proposition at all. It is further the case that theologians would object to such an account as above suggested, if such an account were possible, for they would immediately accuse the

72

account of necessarily committing Christian belief to a reductionist thesis.

Let us now consider other propositions expressed by sentences containing abstract terms as putative subjects and consider what analysis we should offer of such propositions with a view to seeing whether propositions containing 'God' as a putative subject are amenable to such an analysis such that we can say that sentences of the form 'God is F' can be said to express propositions of such a form. The first point to note, following Geach, is that if we do introduce an abstract term then it must always be introduced in relation to something. That is, abstract terms have an incomplete form, they have the form 'F-ness of *y*', as noted in the discussion above and this form itself cannot be analysed into 'F-ness', 'of', '*y*' but remains an unanalysable whole parallel to (e.g.) 'The square root of 4'. That abstract terms when correctly viewed form a non-elementary part of a wider item 'F-ness of *y*' can be seen from the fact that all such terms are derived from concrete predicates. As St Augustine remarks at *De Trinitate* V, 2: 'For as Wisdom is called from being wise, and knowledge from knowing, so also from being is that which is called *essentia*'. The claim that there can be sentences containing abstract nouns as their grammatical subjects which can express propositions about abstract entities, which propositions in turn are irreducible to propositions containing the concrete predicates from which such abstractions are derived, is an impossible one since it denies the very basis on which such abstractions are possible. It was Plato's mistake to think that there could be such irreducible propositions as Geach has beautifully pointed out[39] and, I should contend, Parmenides (in Plato's dialogue of that name) did likewise. Thus such propositions as 'Redness is an eternal object' are nonsensical and for any proposition expressed by a sentence containing the abstract term 'Redness' we must be able to supply an equivalent proposition in terms of the concrete predicate from which such an abstraction is possible. So, citing Geach's example, for 'neither oneness nor manyness is the mark of human nature itself' we have 'Whether there is one man or many men is irrelevant to what X must be if X is a man'. Or again, for 'Happiness is sought after by most men' we have 'Most men seek to be happy'; for 'Wisdom is a quality lacking in most undergraduate revolutionaries' we have 'Most undergraduate

73

revolutionaries are not wise'. As Professor Prior has said:

> We may, for instance, say the same thing with abstract nouns or common ones and either way does equally well. We may, for instance, say 'The people were very happy' or 'The people's happiness was great'. The second sentence isn't 'meaningless' because its subject is an abstraction: on the contrary it means exactly the same as the first. I do insist however that the second sentence does not *add* anything to the first. We are not first given information about happy people and then new information about their happiness – the sentence about their happiness is just another way of telling us about their happiness.[40]

On the basis of these considerations the only analysis which we could offer of theological propositions expressed by sentences of the form under consideration would be an analysis which demanded that for 'God' we could substitute 'The God of x' which is impossible for reasons already offered earlier. However, a protest might be registered against the thesis that any abstract term must be renderable in the form 'The F-ness of y' together with the correlative thesis that all propositions expressed by sentences containing such abstract terms must be reducible to propositions containing the concrete predicates from which such abstractions are derived, on the grounds that there are some sentences which certainly seem to have the use of expressing propositions about abstractions, which abstractions are not exponible in the form *The F-ness of y* and which propositions are not reducible as above required. For example, consider the following:

    (i) Love is stronger than death
   (ii) Love overcometh all things
  (iii) Wisdom is more to be desired than much fine gold
  (iv) Happiness is that which all men seek

It might be pressed that in relation to (i) and (ii) 'Love' is not exponible as 'the love of a', for whilst it is true that Love itself is stronger than death, it might well be false that the love of a (where 'a' takes as values the names of individual people) is stronger than death for all values of a; and again, whilst it is true that Love overcometh all things, it is false that for all values of a, the love of a overcometh all things. Concommit-

74

antly we cannot write for (i), and by parity of reasoning for (ii), 'M, N, O . . . n's love is stronger than death', for all values of a. Again, in relation to (iii), whilst it is true that Wisdom is more to be desired than much fine gold, it might well be false that the wisdom of M, N, O . . . n for all values of a, is more to be desired than much fine gold. One should only seek after Wisdom itself and not after the particular wisdoms of this world. Similar points might be made in relation to (iv) and again, as concerns (iv) it might be said that one should seek after Happiness itself, not the happiness of someone or other or of some particular group of people. Further, to press the point, it might be added that Love, Wisdom and Happiness have certain predicates which hold true of them which cannot hold true of the love of what is named by a value for a, which cannot hold true of the wisdom of what is named by a value for a, and which cannot hold true of the happiness of what is named by a value for a – for example, 'eternal'; 'immutable'; 'incorruptible'; 'ungenerable'. Love is eternal, but the love of Socrates for Xanthippe or the love of David for Jonathan is temporal, changeable, corruptible and certainly came into existence. Wisdom is eternal, but the wisdom of Socrates had a beginning and an end in time, was open to change, was certainly corruptible (and *was* corrupted by the Sophists) and came into existence; likewise the wisdom of the ancient Egyptians and Babylonians. Happiness is eternal, immutable, etc., but the happiness of Ruth endured but for a season and likewise that of any other human being; the happiness of Ruth or Rebecca of old was open to change and corruption and came into existence and went out of existence – unlike Happiness itself.

Faced with the situation (a) that there are certain sentences, such as 'Love is stronger than death' and 'Wisdom is more to be desired than much fine gold', containing abstract nouns as grammatical subjects seemingly expressing propositions about abstractions, which propositions, it is claimed will remain true even if all propositions which on the above thesis they are exponible as are false, and (b) that there are some propositions having abstractions as their putative subjects, which propositions it is claimed are true, but whose predicates could never hold true of the 'individual instances' of those abstractions, are we to say that the former thesis is false? Not at all: a condition of accepting the above cases as counter cases to the original

75

thesis is that in the above cases we have genuine subject–predicate propositions being expressed, but in order for genuine subject–predicate propositions to be so expressed, the question of the *reference* of such terms as 'Love', 'Wisdom', etc., must be one which can be raised and answered sensibly, which, *ex hypothesi*, it cannot since these are precisely abstract terms and one cannot ask for the reference of an abstract term. The only way in which it would be possible for the question of reference to be raised would be to construe such abstract terms as proper names, which construction is impossible since proper names, whilst requiring the prior introduction of predicates which can furnish at least a criterion of continued identity for the continued use of the name, are in no sense abstractions from such predicates. Further, if we were, *per impossible* to construe such abstract terms as proper names and initially raise the question of reference we could never in principle answer it since we have no possible means of specifying any supposed reference. Any specification of reference must include a term which, at the very least, supplies us with a criterion of continued identity, but there is nothing which could so furnish us in the case of supposed 'eternal' objects. It might be replied that we *can* specify the supposed reference in the following way. We might say (e.g.) 'Love is a *virtue* which is such that . . .' or 'Wisdom is a *virtue* which is such that . . .'; but to say that Wisdom or Love is a virtue is *not* to specify what Wisdom or Love is. Telling someone that Wisdom or Love is a virtue will not help him to pick out a case of wisdom or love, let alone Wisdom itself or Love itself. To say that Wisdom or Love is a virtue is distinctly *not* to tell us 'anything about' Wisdom or Love, but to say that Wisdom or Love ought to be pursued for its own sake and to say that Wisdom or Love ought to be pursued for its own sake is simply to say that one ought to be wise or loving and to be wise or loving, i.e. to live a wise or loving life, will bring its own reward. To say, for example, that Love overcometh all things is not to make some true proposition about an eternal entity but to say that anyone who lives a certain kind of life will overcome the many difficulties that beset us in our everyday lives. To say that Love is stronger than death is equally not to make some true proposition about an eternal entity but to say that anyone who lives a loving life will overcome that spiritual death of being bound by our own interest which besets us all.

76

Parallel accounts can be offered of the other examples I considered concerning Wisdom.

6. It is thus my conclusion that:

(a) In so far as 'God' is an abstract term and in so far as Christianity demands that it be such (as I have argued that such is the case in St Thomas's doctrine that in God *suppositum* and nature are to be identified) then sentences containing 'God' as grammatical subject cannot be construed as either:

(i) expressing propositions of a subject–predicate type

(ii) expressing propositions of a general existential type of the form $(\exists x)(Gx.$ for all y, Gy only if y = x. Fx) since such an account would require that 'God' be an ordinary descriptive predicable term

(iii) expressing propositions of identity

(iv) expressing propositions of the form 'a, b, c, . . . is F^1. is F' by parallel with and extension on those propositions which propositions expressed by sentences containing abstract terms are exponible as. To get a parallel to such propositions in the 'God' case, for, for example, 'God is good' we should have to have 'A, B, C, . . . (where 'A', 'B', 'C', . . . are the proper names of individuals) are divine and good' in general 'A, B, C, . . .are divine and F', where 'F' takes as values the adjectival term equivalents of those abstract terms putatively signifying the divine attributes. But it does not seem possible to get such a parallel since we cannot substitute 'divine' for 'God'. There are predicates which, it is claimed, hold true of God which do not hold true of that which is nevertheless truly divine (e.g. '—— is three persons in one substance'), but it does not hold true of the persons of the Trinity (who are truly divine) that they are severely three persons in one substance. Again, there are predicates which hold true of that which is truly divine (e.g. Jesus Christ) which do not hold true of God himself (of the Godhead), for example, '—— was begotten of the Father'; '—— was made in the true image of the Father'. The thesis that sentences of the form: 'God is F' or 'God is infinitely F' (where 'God' is an abstract term) express propositions of the form (iv) above would commit one to saying that all sentences which were previously thought to express propositions 'about' God (the Godhead) must now be construed as expressing propositions about the three persons of the Trinity conjointly;

in other words that all propositions about the Godhead are exponsible as propositions about the three persons of the Trinity in the way in which all propositions containing abstractions as their putative subjects are exponsible in terms of propositions mentioning individuals or at least having indirect reference to individuals and containing concrete predicates. But, as I have indicated, there are some propositions concerning God (the Godhead) which are clearly not so exponible and hence one cannot offer (iv) as the appropriate form of proposition expressed.

(v) that since even (iv) fails no adequate account of the form of proposition expressed by sentences of the above form, where 'God' is an abstract term, can be offered.

(b) Whilst 'God' is an abstract term for at least one theology, it is also, we may suspect, treated in such a context as a proper name in that abstract terms are regarded as a species of name (as I expounded in my last section), but (as I there argued) it is impossible to so regard abstract terms. Even so, I surmise that it is for this reason that not all propositions about God, in the sense of the Godhead, are exponible in terms of propositions about the persons of the Trinity taken conjointly.

(c) That in so far as 'God' is a descriptive predicable term then it cannot and necessarily cannot meet the demands placed upon it by the requirement that it be an abstract one.

(d) That therefore 'God', as an item of Christian language, exhibits the incompatible features of (i) being a descriptive predicable (Frege's *Begriffswort*); (ii) being an abstract term; (iii) being a proper name in that it is held that abstract terms are a type of proper name.

(e) That if one raises the question 'What is the form of proposition expressed by sentences of the form "God is F"?', no single answer can be given since "God" has to play different and indeed incompatible roles in Christian language and whatever considerations would lead us to one account are countered by considerations in favour of another which is inconsistent with the first. It might be said that the arguments advanced so far only indicate that no *one* consistent account can be offered, not that *no* account can be offered, for we might be able to offer several different accounts according to whether 'God', as an item of a particular theological or religious language was to

78

be taken as an abstract term, a definite description of a certain kind, a general term of a certain kind, etc. (assuming, for the sake of argument, that there are no fundamental difficulties for such accounts). But if we were to propose a programme of offering different accounts, then we should be talking about *different* terms since no term can be both (e.g.) a proper name and an abstract one; a proper name and a descriptive predicable; an abstract term and a descriptive predicable, and indirectly about *different* types of entity since if some entity *n* is such that it can be the bearer of a name then that entity cannot be an abstraction and if any entity is such that it can be the bearer of a proper name then it cannot be instantiated and if any entity is such that it is an abstraction then it cannot be instantiated. Yet it is to fly in the face of what is commonly held, to fly in the face of '$\tau\grave{\alpha}$ $\phi\alpha\iota\nu\acute{o}\mu\epsilon\nu\alpha$', as Aristotle would say,[41] to hold that, when 'God' occurs in religious or theological language in the Christian tradition, we have a different type of term in differing theologies and certainly to fly in the face of what is commonly held to hold that, when 'God' occurs in such language, according to the context supplied, different and indeed incompatible types of entity are being introduced and talked about. I thus contend that since no single account can be given of the logical status of 'God' and hence, necessarily, no single account of the form of proposition expressed by sentences of the above form, no account can be offered that is consistent with what is commonly held – in short, that 'God' exhibits radically incompatible logics.

4 Some Possible Non-Propositional Accounts of the Role of Sentences of the Form: 'God is F'

I have so far argued that 'God', as an item of Christian language, exhibits different and incompatible logics and hence, I have contended, not only is it not possible to present a single account of the form of proposition expressed by sentences of the 'God is F' form, but also it is not possible to offer several different accounts and yet meet with the requirement that the same term is being introduced into the discourse or the same entity being spoken of. In this chapter I shall investigate a possible rejoinder to these difficulties – namely that it is quite misguided to think that sentences instancing the above form actually have the role of expressing propositions or indeed have the role of making any 'first order' remarks in the Christian system of discourse; rather, they have the function of determining what is *possible* within such a system of discourse.

1. It will be pressed that we shall only see the form such sentences have and only be able to offer an intelligible account of them when we see what their role is in the 'universe of discourse' of religious belief. Sentences of the form I have been considering obviously occur in many different contexts within the 'language game' of the Christian religion, but one central and crucial context in which they so occur, it will be said, is in that part of theological discourse which deals with the 'nature' of God, and, it might be said, in so far as they occur as part of such 'formal' discourse, the role of such sentences is to put forward 'grammatical' remarks, in Wittgenstein's sense of 'grammatical'. Professor Phillips has helpfully expanded on Wittgenstein's sense of 'grammatical remark' as follows:

It makes as little sense to say that God's existence is not a fact as it does to say that God's existence is a fact. In saying something is or is not a fact in this philosophical context, I am not describing the 'something' in question. To say that 'X' is a fact, here, is to say something about the grammar of 'X': it is to indicate what it would and what it would not be sensible to say or do in connection with it. To say that the concept of divine reality does not share this grammar is to reject the possibility of talking about God in the way in which one talks about matters of fact.[1]

Do sentences of the form I am considering have this function in the context I have mentioned? Professor Phillips has stipulated that the use of 'is a matter of fact' which presents us with a grammatical remark concerning the existence of Mars, is a philosophical use and hence it might be thought that since the sentences of the form I am considering do not occur, in the use I am considering, in a philosophical context, they cannot have a grammatical function. However it does not seem to be a necessary condition of a sentence expressing a grammatical remark that it should explicitly occur in a philosophical discussion. It can be seriously argued that Aquinas' thesis that God is not a body is such a remark from the kinds of consideration he puts forward to support it, but this occurs in the context of Natural Theology.[2] If we rewrite sentences of the form I have been considering in the form of 'God is infinitely F', then the suggestion is that such sentences yield grammatical remarks about God; far from having the role of putting forward true propositions concerning God they have the role of determining what can possibly be true or false propositions concerning God. Thus, if we construe (e.g.) 'God is infinitely good' as a comment of grammar on God, this would be to indicate that the reality of God, as regards his goodness, is not like that of man. To say that God is infinitely good, on this account, indicates that what it makes sense to say concerning the goodness of man does not hold concerning the divine goodness. Concerning the goodness of man we say that it might fail or lose its strength, that it is determined by circumstances. In contrast, it makes no sense to say that God might fail (and has failed, is now failing, or will fail) to be good to one; the divine goodness (logically) can never fail. Again it makes no sense to say that God's goodness might lose its strength or that it is determined by circumstances.

81

However things seem and *however* things turn out, God's goodness *cannot* fail – as the hymn has it: 'The King of Love my shepherd is, whose goodness faileth never', 'faileth never' in the sense that nothing could possibly constitute such a failure. If we are tempted to say that God's goodness has failed us in that we have been in one disaster after another or because those whom we love have fared ill in this life, then we are steeped in misunderstanding. In this 'universe of discourse' nothing can possibly constitute God's goodness failing or waning or being governed by circumstances.

It will here be retorted that if nothing *can* constitute God's goodness failing then the notion of 'failure' has no sense in this discourse, to which it may be replied: 'Precisely so'. However the objector will continue that if nothing can constitute God's goodness failing and the notion of 'failing' has no sense in this connection, then equally, nothing *can* constitute God's goodness operating either and hence the notion of 'God's goodness operating' has no sense either. If it is part of the 'grammar' of the goodness of God, or follows from that 'grammar', that nothing can possibly constitute God's goodness failing, then it must also follow from that 'grammar' that nothing can constitute God's goodness operating either and if nothing can possibly constitute this then the notion of God's goodness operating is itself a nonsensical one, for the sense of 'operating' is dependent upon the sense of the notion of 'failing to operate'; they are correlatives. Yet no Christian would want to deny that the notion of God's goodness operating is one which is present in Christian discourse, even though it might be acknowledged that in some cases it is a problematic matter as to what constitutes God's goodness operating. Thus, if we construe 'God is infinitely good' as a remark of 'grammar' indicating that it makes no sense to say that (e.g.) God's goodness might fail, then we have to maintain that the notion of God's goodness operating in the world, whatever might be said to constitute this, is a nonsensical one. I do not see how any Christian could maintain such a position; the 'grammatical' construction of such a sentence as 'God is infinitely good' leads one to, at the very least, unpalatable consequences and strictly to paradoxical ones.

It might well be commented that this argument, which is obviously based on arguments put forward in an earlier age by

82

Professor Flew, depends for its validity upon the thesis that 'failing to operate' and 'operating' are necessarily correlatives irrespective of context: this is true and can only be denied at the cost of ignoring an important logical point. Granted, it is possible that in various 'universes of discourse' (language games) what constitutes X operating or failing to operate will be different and in this way the truth conditions of propositions containing such phrases will be different as between those language games, but this concession does not mitigate against the above argument – rather it supposes that in such areas of discourse the distinction between 'operating' and 'failing to operate' is itself in operation, which has to be denied on the construction of 'God is infinitely F' as remarks of grammar concerning God.

Similar comments apply to the construction of 'God is infinitely merciful' as grammatical. On this construction nothing *can* constitute God's mercy failing, unlike the case in regard to human mercy. A merciful man might cease to be merciful to us for some offences often committed; doing such and such *this* time might be an occasion for him to restrain his mercy. It will be said by those who advocate the 'grammatical' interpretation that God's mercy is not like this; it is not this *kind* of mercy. Nothing can constitute an occasion for God to restrain his mercy, and therefore, the notion of God restraining his mercy is an unintelligible one.[3] But, it must be commented, if the notion of God restraining his mercy is an unintelligible one *so* is that of God showing forth his mercy; these are correlatives. We cannot fail to have one and have the other. Yet it cannot be denied that in Christian discourse the notion of God showing forth his mercy is one in current and perpetual use. The 'grammatical' construction of 'God is infinitely merciful' commits one, at the best, to the unpalatable and paradoxical view that the notion of God showing forth his mercy is a (strictly) nonsensical notion; at the worst, it forces one into the nonsense of having to say that it is possible for the concept of God's mercy never failing to be introduced and indeed having been introduced without the correlative notion of God's mercy failing being introduced or having been introduced. If someone says 'That is how things are in the language game of the Christian religion' then such a 'language game' is open to the charge of unintelligibility on this formal count concerning correlatives. What constitutes 'showing mercy' and 'failing to show mercy' will vary as between 'language games' and hence the truth conditions of propositions containing such predicates will vary as between those 'language games', but the introduction of the notion of 'showing mercy' formally demands the introduction of 'failing to show mercy' *whatever* the 'language game' in question.

A variant on the original theme might here be suggested, namely that treating 'God is infinitely merciful' (in general, 'God is infinitely F') as a remark of grammar does not indicate that it is *nonsense* to speak of God's goodness or mercy failing; it is *possible* so to speak but that either (i) nothing could constitute God's mercy (goodness, etc.) failing, i.e. it could never in principle be true that God's mercy (goodness, etc.) has failed or will fail; (ii) we cannot know what would constitute God's mercy (goodness, etc.) failing; or (iii) we are not in a position to know what would constitute God's mercy (goodness, etc.) failing. If (i) is put forward then one is open to the charge of introducing a concept which can have no application and hence is void – necessarily void, as can be seen by the fact that it is a requirement of any (genuine) concept whatsoever being introduced into discourse that it can, in theory, have application, i.e. that it can, in theory, form part of a true proposition. Thus to say that nothing *can* constitute God's mercy (goodness, etc.) failing, that this concept (in theory) can never have application, is tantamount to saying that it cannot be sensibly introduced and hence we are back to the same problem as faced us above. To put forward (ii) obviously gives rise to the paradox that if it is sensible to speak of God's mercy (goodness, etc.) failing but we cannot know what would constitute such a failure, then there is no means of determining what would constitute God's mercy (goodness, etc.) operating either. We may *say* that we know that such and such constitutes God's mercy, etc., operating, but the truth is, on *this* account, that we are not in a position either to claim such knowledge or to disclaim it. To put forward (iii) gives rise to a similar paradox, for if we are not in a position to know what would constitute God's mercy (goodness, etc.) failing, then, equally, we are not in a position to know that what passes for God's goodness operating is, in truth, God's goodness operating or not.

Thus the construction of such sentences of the form I am

considering as 'grammatical' whilst potentially a possible construction entails, at the best, unpalatable and paradoxical results, at the worst, unintelligible ones. A further point on this proposed construction must be noted in the light of the earlier discussion concerning the logical status of 'God'. This construction will only work if we take 'God' as an ordinary descriptive predicable (general term), for the 'grammatical remark' has the form: 'Whatever is God is infinitely F', but only in some uses does 'God' so operate, as I have argued earlier and further in the context of that part of the *Summa Theologica* in which Aquinas discusses the relation of the 'Divine attributes' to God, it is necessary *not* to so construe 'God', otherwise no satisfactory account of the doctrine that God is his nature or essence can be offered which answers to the thought of Aquinas. Yet it is precisely in such a context that the 'grammatical' account has *prima facie* plausibility.

2. It might be held that the function of sentences of the form under consideration is not that of putting forward propositions or 'grammatical remarks' in the above discussed sense but of presenting us with a picture or set of pictures. This would seem to be the implication of some of Wittgenstein's comments in his *Lectures and Conversations on Religious Belief*.[4] He writes:

> The word 'God' is amongst the earliest learnt – pictures and catechisms, etc. But not with the same consequences as with pictures of aunts. I wasn't shown [that which the picture pictured].
> The word is used like a word representing a person. God sees, rewards, etc.[5]

The implications of these remarks are:

(a) The sense in which the word 'God' is a picture is certainly not the sense in which the picture of my aunt is a picture, for in this latter case it would make sense to say that one could be presented with the aunt; in the 'God' case there is nothing which could constitute being presented with God. In the 'God' case the picture is the totality. This is borne out by Wittgenstein's further comments (p. 63):

> You could imagine that religion was taught by the means of

85

these pictures (e.g. Michelangelo's 'Creation')[6] 'Of course, we can only express ourselves by means of picture'.

If a religious person says this, Wittgenstein comments 'This is rather queer . . . I could show Moore the pictures of a tropical plant. There is a technique of comparison between the picture and plant'. The implication of this is that there could be no technique of comparison between the picture of God in Michelangelo's 'Creation' and the Deity. This is carried through in Wittgenstein's following remark:

> If I showed him the picture of Michelangelo and said: 'Of course I can't show you the real thing, only the picture' . . . The absurdity is, I've never taught him the technique of using this picture.

Here the point clearly is that 'Of course . . . only the picture' is absurd since in this case the distinction between the real thing and the picture cannot be drawn, i.e. cannot be sensibly introduced; the use of the picture is such (it is claimed) that it does not permit the distinction. Professor Phillips has reiterated this point in his discussion of Flew on the question of whether one can witness one's own funeral; Flew has, he claims, shown a misunderstanding since he does think religious pictures have the use of being pictures *of*.[7]

(b) To say 'God rewards, sees, etc.', is not like saying that a person sees, rewards, etc., since there is a set of questions which can be asked and a set of inferences which can be made concerning a person seeing, rewarding, etc., which cannot (respectively) be asked or made in the case of God seeing or rewarding, for one cannot ask of the items within a picture or of the picture itself either (a) what one can ask of what is pictured (in the case of representational art), or (b) what is symbolised (in the case of non-representational art).

Now both (a) and (b) assume that (i) words represent (Wittgenstein writes: 'The word ['God'] is used like a word representing a person'); (ii) that some sentences (at least) can be regarded as pictures or (iii) what some sentences (at least) can be said to express are pictures. I shall first argue that these assumptions are false and then consider two recent attempts to develop the 'picture' theory, exposing, I hope, the fatal flaws in each and raise the question as to how such theories could cope with instances of the form of sentence I have been considering.

It is clearly false that proper names either represent, depict, portray, symbolise or image, yet items within a picture can variously be said to represent, depict, portray, symbolise or image. We cannot ask what 'Socrates' in its use as the proper name of the fifth century philosopher *represents*. The proper name 'Socrates' does not represent Socrates, it names him or, on a given occasion of use, refers to him. Again, the name does not in any way depict or portray Socrates, as opposed to name him; a proper name is in no sense a kind of miniature portrait of what is named. Neither does the name symbolise what is named though there may be something symbolic in that a particular proper name is given to a particular individual. Neither is the name 'Socrates' an image of Socrates – the name 'Socrates' cannot even meaningfully be said to look like the man Socrates. Further, not only is it false that proper names represent, portray, symbolise, etc., but they cannot meaningfully be said so to do. It is not part of their 'grammar' that they can be thus spoken of. Further, common nouns, adjectives, verbs and other parts of speech cannot be said to take on such functions as those above mentioned. For example, the noun 'cat' in the English sentence 'I have just seen a cat' can in some circumstances of use identify what I see, in other circumstances specify what I see, in other circumstances describe what I see. However, an identification is not a representation nor even a peculiar sort of representation; indeed the very notion of 'representation' presupposes the identification of what is purportedly represented on a given occasion of representation. An identification is either correct or incorrect; a representation is neither correct nor incorrect but either good or poor, adequate or inadequate, (possibly) clear or unclear. Further a specification is not a representation. A specification may be precise or imprecise, accurate or inaccurate, adequate or inadequate but neither good nor poor and one cannot ask what a specification represents. Again a description is not a representation. A description may apply or fail to apply, be satisfied or fail to be satisfied and one cannot ask what a description represents. On the other hand a representation neither applies or fails to apply, is satisfied or fails to be satisfied and it is the case that one can ask of any A which has the status of a representation

87

what it represents. Further, an identification is not a depiction or a portrayal, neither is a specification: one cannot ask what any given identification depicts or portrays or what any given specification depicts or portrays. Neither an identification nor a specification is a kind of drawing or a kind of portrait; indeed the very idea of a drawing or portrait in at least representational art presupposes the idea of identification. It might, however, be claimed that a description is a kind of portrait, a verbal portrait. Nevertheless there is an important difference here in that at least a description can be said to be satisfied or fail to be satisfied or to apply or fail to apply; a portrait cannot be so spoken of and in that we might want to speak of a set of descriptions as constituting a verbal portrait of an individual this is an analogous extension of the concept of a portrait – as witness the fact that we speak of a *verbal* portrait, whereas we do not speak of a pictorial portrait, a 'pictorial' portrait is a portrait *period*. To speak of a verbal portrait of an actual individual is to speak of an artistically arranged set of true propositions concerning that individual or of one proposition containing many descriptions which are satisfied by or correctly apply to that individual. But a portrait of Socrates is not a true proposition concerning Socrates, neither does it apply to nor is it satisfied by Socrates. To speak of a verbal portrait of a non-actual entity, i.e. an imaginary one, is to speak of an artistically arranged set of pretence propositions or one such pretence proposition containing many pretence descriptions concerning a pretended reference. Again, an identification is not a symbolisation. In identifying something we do not symbolise it, neither in symbolising something do we identify it; indeed in symbolising something we presuppose identification in order to specify what is so symbolised. Neither is a specification of something a symbolisation of that thing; in responding to the injunction 'Specify what you see' by saying 'I see a black cat', I do not symbolise the cat. The same holds true of describing something and of the description, and to symbolise something in the sense of producing a symbol of that thing is not to describe the thing; indeed the possibility of producing a symbol presupposes in at least some cases the possibility of description and we don't produce a description *for* anything. In concluding these present remarks, it is sufficient to say that neither an identification, specification or description is an image, for an image has the *look* of the original. An image is an eikon and at least in the same genre as the original,[8] but words used in identifying, specifying and describing cannot even meaningfully be said to look like what they respectively identify, specify, or describe.

In the above discussion I have only taken an example of one part of speech, viz. an example of a common noun, and considered its possible functions, claiming that such words in their possible typical employments cannot take on those roles or functions which signs which are possible elements in the vocabulary of art can be said to take on. Similar points could be made in relation to other parts of speech; I shall not trouble the reader with the detailed working out of such points since for present purposes one type of counter case will suffice to refute the thesis that words can be regarded as representations, portraits, etc. To counter another possible line of thought, it is not the case that words can be regarded as representations of thought elements, or as symbols for thought elements, or as images of thought elements since the relation between a thought and its expression is a non-contingent one. Thoughts are necessarily expressed *in* a language and hence they cannot be represented *by*, symbolised *by*, or imaged *by*, any item in any language, as opposed to expressed *in* items of a language.

It might be contended that although words cannot be regarded as representations, images, symbols or portraits, nevertheless sentences can be regarded as a kind of picture and/or what sentences can be said to express either are or at least can be regarded as a picture or kind of picture. However, since sentences are ordered sets or arrangements of words – that is, ordered according to syntactical (grammatical) rules – and words cannot be regarded as representations, portraits, symbols or images, then sentences cannot be regarded as ordered sets or arrangements of such representations, portraits, symbols, or images, as a picture can be said to be a function of such an ordered set or arrangement. It might be thought that it is valid to make the following point, namely, that whilst we can ask of any purported sentence in language L whether it is meaningful in that language, we cannot ask of any set of (pictorial) representations, images, or symbols whether it is meaningful in anything like a parallel fashion. It is not so valid; there are analogies to be drawn but the drawing of such analogies does not affect my previous argument. We can ask of any putative sentence whether it is meaningful in language L in the following senses: (a) whether it contains as its component parts signs which are words in that language L, and (b) whether it obeys the rules of grammar and syntax in that language L. Correspondingly we can say of sentence S that it is meaningful in language L in that it contains as its constituent parts signs which are words in that language and in that it obeys the rules of grammar and syntax for that language. By parallel it certainly seems possible to ask of any set of representations, images or symbols whether it is a meaningful whole in a particular language of Art. For any such set to be meaningful in a sense corresponding to (a) above will be for it to contain as elements signs which are recognised symbols in a given language of art R (say Representational Art); for any such set to be meaningful in a sense corresponding to (b) above will be for those symbols to be arranged in accordance with the 'syntactical' rules implicit in that language of art R. It thus seems possible to draw at least some parallel between (i) a sentence and (ii) a set of representations or symbols, organised according to certain artistic principles analogous to syntactical principles in written or spoken language and both can be said to be meaningful in at least the senses expounded. But from this it does not follow that sentences *are* a kind of picture both for the reason already offered and for the further reason that what corresponds to the sentence at the artistic level is not a picture but an ordered collection of symbols. A picture is not simply such an ordered collection or arrangement of such accepted symbols but a function of such a collection or arrangement, so what would correspond to a picture in a natural language would not be a sentence but a function of a sentence (it is worth noting here that in the *Tractatus* it is the proposition, not the sentence, which is thought of as a picture).

I shall now argue that although we have been able to pursue some analogy between sentences and ordered collections of symbols, etc. in an artistic language, we cannot pursue the analogy any further such that we can say that what sentences can be said to express are pictures in some sense.

We can ask of any (type) sentence what on a given occasion of use (token instance) its function is and we can also ask of any ordered arrangement of symbols, images, etc. (type) what on

90

any given occasion its function is; but the possible functions of sentences are not the possible functions of such sets of symbols. For example, a sentence (in the indicative mood) can be used to state, propound, or assert. An ordered arrangement of pictorial symbols which has the function of a picture might be said to represent, portray, depict, or symbolise, but to represent, portray, depict or symbolise is neither to state, propound, or assert. Statements, propositions or assertions are possibly true or false, but representations, whilst they may be good or poor, true to life or distorted, well executed or poorly executed, are not possibly either true or false; depictions, whilst they might be clear, apt, good or vivid, are not possibly true or false; portrayals, whilst they might be said to be a true likeness or a poor likeness, good or distorting, character revealing or bland, are not possibly true or false; a symbolisation may be adequate or inadequate, revealing or unrevealing, confusing or apt, but not possibly true or false and to symbolise is distinctly not to state, assert or propound.

It may be thought that I have omitted one important type of case in discussing the possible functions of indicative sentences, which type of case it would be distinctly pertinent to discuss here, namely that role which certain sentences have in certain contexts, i.e. that of making 'grammatical remarks' in Wittgenstein's sense. Grammatical remarks, in this sense, are neither statements, assertions, or propositions; they are not possibly either true or false but determine what can be either true or false in the language for which they are grammatical remarks. They can be said to *show* something in the way in which the 'internal' properties of an object can be said to *show* something about an object (cf. *Tractatus* 2.01231). Cannot therefore certain pictures (which cannot possibly be either true or false) have the possibility of playing this role, especially if we add the further consideration that pictures *show* as opposed to state, assert, or propound? Strictly speaking it cannot be *pictures* which could have such a role; rather, if any case can be made out at all here it will be that certain ordered sets or arrangements of pictorial symbols can play this role, as it is sentences which can play the role of making grammatical remarks. Further, we cannot argue (as here suggested) that since pictures can be neither true nor false then there is a parallel to be drawn with grammatical remarks, since whilst there is

91

no sense in which pictures can be either true or false it can be maintained that 'grammatical remarks', whilst they cannot be held to be true or false statements, propositions, assertions *within* a given system of discourse, are nevertheless axiomatically true *for* that system of discourse. Again, even granted that we could ignore my first comment here, pictures could only have the possibility of playing this role that grammatical remarks play if pictures could be said to show something in a way parallel to that in which grammatical remarks are held to show something. But pictures do *not* show in such a parallel fashion; indeed the sense in which pictures show is a different sense.[9] Even the much courted example of the Last Judgement cannot be said to have such a role. It cannot determine what propositions are possible in Christian discourse or even one area of such discourse; rather it presupposes that certain propositions *are* possible in order for it to have significance for us. It follows from these considerations, or rather is implicit in these considerations, that no case can be made out for the suggestion that, since it is not necessary that every sentence (in the indicative mood) has the role of asserting, stating, propounding, some sentences at least can be regarded as pictures if they have the role of showing since (a) the sense in which a picture shows is not that in which a sentence may be said to show; and (b) the truth that some sentences have the role of showing in the sense of being grammatical remarks is not a sufficient condition of their being regarded as pictures Grammatical remarks are not pictures nor can they possibly be.

Having argued (i) that one cannot regard sentences as pictures and (ii) what sentences can be said to express as pictures or what some sentences *show* as pictures, I shall now turn to the attempt by Professor Phillips to develop Wittgenstein's suggestions.[10] In this development certain sentences are to be regarded as the pictorial expressions of a belief, which 'picture' has a role in the life of the believer. This development therefore subscribes to the false doctrine that some sentences at least can be regarded as pictorial expressions either in the sense of being regarded as ordered arrangements of symbols or as pictures. Granted the truth of what I have argued above, the only way in which it seems possible to discuss this development seriously is to draw a distinction between what a sentence can *express*, viz. a proposition, statement, assertion, and what a sentence

92

can *show*, on the one hand, and what a sentence can *present*, on the other, such that we can argue that some sentences whilst not being pictorial representations or expressing pictures nevertheless *present* us with certain pictures. It is only by some such tenuous distinction that any serious discussion of this development is possible; we need some serious discussion here since this is the most worked out account of Wittgenstein suggestions of which I, at least, am aware.

Phillips does not discuss sentences of the form I am considering nor particular examples of such sentences, but considers such 'pictures' as 'We shall meet after death', 'The eye of God sees everything' and the Last Judgement. The relating of the two former cases with the latter without any apologia makes it clear that Phillips does regard such sentences or, at the most, the beliefs they express as pictures (the latter cannot be unreservedly held in the light of his later remarks to be discussed). Taking as a starting point an illuminating example – the visitation of Scrooge – he argues that the role of this vision in Scrooge's life is a means of reflecting on his life as a whole.[11] Such a vision has the role of reflecting on and re-orientating his whole way of living. Similarly, as concerns the belief that we shall all meet beyond the grave he comments:

> Such a picture may itself be an expression of the belief that people should act towards each other, not according to the status and prestige that people have acquired or failed to acquire, during the course of their lives, but as children of God in the equality which death will reveal.[12]

And again, in relation to the 'Last Judgement' he says: 'This picture plays the role of constantly admonishing me or I always think of it' (Wittgenstein op. cit. p. 56). I commented above that we could not unreservedly say that Phillips holds that it is the *beliefs* which are pictures; this is borne out here in his view that the picture is or may be the *expression* of the belief.

Can we take particular instances of the form of sentence I am discussing (e.g. 'God is loving' or 'God is infinitely loving'; 'God is good' or 'God is infinitely good') in a parallel fashion, namely as presenting a picture having a certain function? (We cannot talk of such sentences either *being* pictures or *expressing* pictures for reasons previously offered.) There are many obstacles to so doing; I shall discuss these first and then go on

93

to raise further inadequacies of the general thesis I take Phillips to be advocating.

(a) How do we specify the picture so presented by such a sentence? Is God to be taken as a loving or infinitely loving man? Clearly not, since there are certain predicates which it is held are true of God and which indeed are held to be part of his 'essence' which cannot possibly be true of human beings, viz. 'eternal', 'necessarily existent', 'immutable', 'transcendent'. It might be replied that this objection does not hold for it is not the case that a picture has to be able to take on those predicates which that which is pictured takes on and, indeed, necessarily not the case; otherwise we should end up having to say that a picture of Socrates is a miniature Socrates, an entity of the same type as Socrates, but in a 'reduced' form, which is plainly absurd. Whilst this reply is correct it does not help here for three reasons. First, according to Phillips' account (following Wittgenstein),[13] the question of what the picture is a picture *of* cannot be raised and therefore the picture itself must somehow 'include' all those attributes traditionally attributed to God, which leaves us with the question of what the X is which is pictured in terms of being F or infinitely F. Just this question seems impossible to answer for all the usual answers, viz. a person, a god, a spirit, or a being, break down in various ways for reasons already offered. Secondly, even if we were to radically alter the thesis such that we talk in terms of images and say that sentences of the form 'God is F' (or 'God is infinitely F') are 'really' writable as (e.g.) 'Jesus Christ is F (or infinitely F)' and sentences of this form present us with images of the Godhead (on the principle that Christ is *Imago Dei*), we are still up against what seem to be insuperable objections, even allowing that there is or might be a sense in which a sentence can *present* us with an image, as opposed to a sentence *being* a kind of image or an ordered arrangement of images, since (i) 'God is F' (or 'God is infinitely F') is not writable as 'Jesus Christ is F' ('Jesus Christ is infinitely F') for there are some true propositions about the Godhead which are false as concerns Christ (e.g. that God is three in one); and (ii) the philosophical problem arises as to in what sense Christ can be said to present us with 'a true and faithful image of God' if either the Godhead (the original) is unknowable or if the Godhead is infinite.[14] Thirdly, in terms of traditional Christianity,

94

such sentences as 'God is the loving shepherd' and 'God is the just judge' are held to present us with a picture in the sense of a parable,[15] but this is in *contrast* to such sentences of the form I am now considering, viz. such sentences must be regarded as expressing something which is non-pictorally true in order for such 'parables' to be possible. We cannot take *all* sentences having God as their putative subject as parables or having the role of parables, otherwise the notion of 'parable' would lose its sense in this context. Our Lord did not speak to everyone in parables.

(b) Even if it were possible to give a specification of the picture so 'presented' by such sentences, the further problem arises as to what the function of the picture so presented is. It might be suggested that we can at least do this for some sentences of the above form. For example, it might be suggested that in the case of 'God is loving', where this is renderable as 'God is infinitely loving', the function of the picture presented by such a sentence is to reflect the belief or present the belief that Love has no bounds, or to reflect the belief or present the belief that we should love one another whatever happens. In the case of 'God is merciful', where this is renderable as 'God is infinitely merciful', the function of the picture presented by such a sentence is to reflect the belief or present the belief that we should always and under any circumstances forgive them that trespass against us. In the case of 'God is good', where this is renderable as 'God is infinitely good', the function of the picture presented by such a sentence is to reflect or present the belief that we should pursue the good life and eschew that which is evil, and that we should do this even when this involves self degradation and condemnation.

Such accounts however give rise to the question 'How is it *decidable* that the 'pictures' presented by such sentences *have* such roles?' Any attempt to answer this question must lead us back to certain further inadequacies of Professor Phillips' position. Phillips gives us no clue on decision procedure in relation to his own accounts of the roles which the picture of (i) the Last Judgement and (ii) the family reunited in Heaven, have. It is pertinent here to ask 'How *does* he decide that the picture that 'We shall all meet beyond the grave' is or may be the expression (presentation) of the belief that 'people should act towards one another . . . as children of God in the equality

95

which death will reveal' (ibid., p. 66)? No decision procedure is put forward or advocated. To invoke the slogan 'Look to the use' is no help here for precisely the use of the 'picture' is in question. Further, even in Phillips could provide us with a decision procedure such that one could decide whether or not the accounts offered above are correct accounts of the function of the picture presented by the sentences there mentioned, we are up against a further difficulty, namely that on Phillips' account thus far the picture is the expression of a belief which can be specified *independently* of the picture. Indeed he gives us a purported example of such an independent specification when he says that 'We shall all meet beyond the grave' is or may be the expression of the belief that people should act towards each other as children of God in the equality which death will reveal and such an independent specification is indicated when he says:

> One's presence as observer in the religious picture (of imagining oneself witnessing one's own funeral)[16] is an expression of how a person can reflect on his life as a whole.[17]

However, it might be objected that the first passage mentioned does not give us an *independent* specification since it invokes the idea of 'children of God' and this itself is part of the religious picture; but if this objection be conceded Phillips cannot be said to have given us an account of the role of the picture 'We shall all meet beyond the grave', for an account of the role of the picture cannot be given in terms either explicitly or implicitly involving a reference to an item in the picture or implied by an item or items in the picture. It might be further objected that no such independent specification is indicated by the second passage just cited; but it surely must be since in order for the 'picture' of Scrooge witnessing his own funeral to have the role of reflecting on his life, then such an independent account must at least be givable if not actually given – otherwise nothing could possibly constitute the picture either reflecting or being a way of reflecting. In the 'Scrooge' case it is not difficult to supply an account – 'the "picture" is a reflection of the truth that Scrooge had been mean, grasping, selfish (and so on for the list of all the vices of Scrooge)'.

Granted the account so far, the problem which specifically arises in the religious cases is obvious, namely it is simply false, as far as traditional Christianity is concerned, to say that religious beliefs are a way of expressing (in my terms, a way of presenting) or a way of reflecting on some independently specifiable truth or truths. The accounts offered above of such sentences as 'God is loving' ('God is infinitely loving'), etc., *even if* they could overcome all the previous hurdles, would crucially falter at this one.

However, the above account of Professor Phillips' programme does not represent the whole account, for later on (ibid. p. 70) he contends that the 'pictures' are not poor substitutes for other ways of saying things – often there is no other or better way of stating what the 'pictures' say and

> The picture is not a picturesque way of saying something else: it says what it says and when the picture dies something dies with it.

(ibid. p. 77–8). He here cites Wittgenstein (op. cit. p. 72): 'The whole *weight* may be in the picture'. From these passages it would seen that *in principle* no *independent* account of what is believed can be offered. If this is so Phillips has freed himself from the objection raised immediately above at the expense of producing an internally inconsistent account of religious beliefs as pictures or, more correctly, of religious sentences as expressing (presenting) beliefs in a pictorial form. Now, even ignoring this internal inconsistency and taking it that his true position is reflected in his later remarks, even then we seem to have an unsurmountable problem in addition to those already raised earlier, viz. if no independent account of what is believed can in principle be given, how is it *possible* to say that the role of these 'pictures' is to *express* (*present*) anything or is the *expression of* (*presentation of*) anything? – or to *reflect* anything or be the *reflection of* anything? Yet *that* the role or use of religious 'pictures' is to reflect or express something or other is essential to Phillips' position; even in his example from the Ho dirge, which appears in the context of his later remarks (pp. 70–1) he writes:

> . . . as long as people can sing the song the dead have not deserted them. The song is an expression of that truth.

In this case we bring out the force of such a picture (the song) in saying that its role is to express the truth that the dead have not deserted those who sing the song. So even here the truth *is*

97

independently specifiable and hence Phillips cannot consistently maintain his own position as latterly expressed.

In the light of these considerations I conclude that in so far as Wittgenstein's suggestion that religious remarks are to be taken as pictures having a certain role or function has been worked out by Professor Phillips, even if we can get over the initial difficulties implicit in the idea that a sentence is a kind of picture, the account is at the worst internally inconsistent and at best fraught with, as far as I can judge, unsurmountable difficulties and cannot be used as an illuminating way of giving an account of sentences of the form I have as the topic of my investigation.

I said earlier that I should discuss two recent attempts to develop the 'picture' theory of religious language. The second attempt is that offered by Dr Hudson in his paper 'Some Remarks on Wittgenstein's Account of Religious Belief'.[18]

Dr Hudson helpfully distinguishes between two senses of 'the use to which the picture is put'. The first sense is the use of a picture which is given in or is definitive of the religion in question. He gives as an example:

> It is given in or definitive of Christianity that from the picture, God the Father, the conclusion should be drawn that he regards all men with goodwill, but not the conclusion that He is their physical progenitor.

On his account to use this picture with understanding, must be a matter of recognising what is said or done in a religion as logically connected with what there is taken as fundamental, namely the picture in use. He says of the use which is given or definitive:

> . . . if, for example, I, as a Christian, have not merely learned to say 'God loves us' but to say it with understanding, then, at a minimum, I recognise it as logically entailed by the picture, God the Father (assuming that picture to be fundamental to Christianity).

I find this account unsatisfactory for the following reasons:

(i) Even if it is possible to construe a phrase as presenting a picture, as opposed to a phrase either being a picture or expressing a picture, it is quite unclear *what* picture we are presented with by such a phrase. If it is replied that it is a misunderstanding to raise the question 'What picture?' then we are forced back on to the former difficulties concerning a form of words being a picture at all.

(ii) As it stands this form of words, if it has a recognisable use at all, is simply the title of the first person of the Trinity. In order for this form of words to be treated as a picture or to be a picture, *even if* we were to allow that sentences can be *regarded as* pictures or *are* pictures, we should at the very least have to reformulate in the form of a sentence (e.g.) 'God is the father of all men', but even on such a reformulation we are still faced with the difficulty raised in (i) above.

(iii) In what sense can 'God the Father', construed as a picture, *entail* any proposition? Only propositions or possibly statements can be said to entail or be entailed by one another. Thus only if (a) 'God the Father' is writable as (e.g.) 'God is the father of all men' and this sentence can in turn, in its use in Christian thought, be said to express a proposition, or, if 'God the Father' can be said to occur as the subject of some proposition and that whole proposition be ennunciated; or (b) if 'God is the father of all men' can be used by someone to make a statement, can the question of entailment arise. Yet if we say that 'God the Father' is expandable to read 'God is the father of all men' and that this sentence in turn can be said to express a proposition or be used by Christians to make a statement, we seem to have rejected the thesis that 'God the Father' is a picture, for part (at least) of the point of saying that 'God the Father' is a picture is that such a form of words, in a suitably expanded form, cannot be used to express a proposition or make a statement; and in any case, in the light of my previous arguments, it cannot be held that pictures either state or propound; they represent, depict, portray, symbolise or image. In no sense can a picture entail a proposition – or for that matter entail anything at all.

(iv) According to Hudson, 'God loves us' is 'entailed' by the picture. This gives rise to the problem as to whether 'God loves us' as so 'entailed' is likewise to be regarded as a picture in the same sense as the original or in a different sense or not at all to be so regarded. *Even if* (in the light of objections to the thesis that sentences can be regarded as pictures) we could possibly construe the original 'God is the father of all men' as 'God is to be regarded as the father of all men (by analogy)', 'God loves us' cannot be regarded as a picture in this same sense since it is totally implausible to write 'God loves us' as 'God is to be regarded as loving us (by analogy)'. A Christian would rightly reply that 'God loves us *period* (as the Americans say); it is not a case of God being regarded as loving us (by analogy)'. If 'God loves us' is to be regarded as a picture in a different sense to that in which the original is a picture, *what* is this sense? If 'God loves us' is not to be regarded as a picture *at all* then what account of this item of language can be offered on Hudson's thesis? He simply talks in terms of 'learning to say "God loves us"', offering no account of what it is so to say. Further, if this item of language is not to be regarded as a picture at all, in what sense could it be 'entailed by' something which *is* a picture on his thesis, even if we could give sense to the concept of 'entailment' in such a situation? The most that Hudson could do here would be to construe the 'original' as an analogical saying and then produce a programme designed to show that analogical sayings can entail non-analogical propositions or statements. However, there is no evidence to the effect that Hudson would even want to say that 'God the Father', expanded to read 'God is the father of all men', is to be regarded as a picture in the sense of an analogical saying. I have only introduced this position as a means to further discussion; strictly it seems that Hudson is firmly wedded to the view that sentences, or at least some sentences, can be regarded as pictures or even *are* pictures and hence is open to all the difficulties involved in that view.

The second sense of 'the use to which the picture is put' which Hudson distinguishes is:

> ... the use which is made of it by adherents of the religion in question when they are reflecting upon their beliefs or interpreting new situations in the light of them.

On this use he comments:

> ... if I reflect upon or discuss, petitionary prayer, let us say, with understanding, then I shall have in mind the *logical connection*[19] between whatever is being thought or said about it, and this picture, God the Father. I shall see the point of view, for instance, that petitionary prayer is unnecessary, when I recognise that this is being said for some such reason

100

as that, God being Father, we do not need to ask him to do us good; or alternatively, of the view that petitionary prayer is essential, when I recognise this as being said for some such reason as that, God being Father, we need to effect our side of a personal relationship with him and petitionary prayer is the way to do it.

One must ask 'What is the "logical connection" here?' The only logical connection mentioned is that of 'logical entailment', by which Hudson must simply mean 'entailment', for entailment is solely a logical connection, or more strictly, a logical relation. There is no such thing as *non*-logical entailment; yet, as I have argued, pictures, not being propositions or statements cannot be said to entail at all. Hence Hudson's second sense of 'the use to which the picture is put' cannot be coherently expounded short of him developing some special sense of 'logical connection' which is not that of entailment; but this he fails to do.[20] We are thus, unfortunately, none the wiser from these accounts as to what is minimal in understanding a religion, yet it was at least part of Dr Hudson's aim to make us wiser in this matter as is clear from the following:

What I wish to say then is this: understanding the use of the picture which is definitive of a religion, or the use to which it is put in continuing reflection or discussion within that religion, is in both cases a matter of seeing the logical connection between what is being said and what is logically fundamental, namely the picture itself. I am sure that there is far more to understanding a religion than this. All I want to say is that there is at least this. (ibid. p. 39)

The internal difficulties of the above two accounts apart and the prior difficulties which I raised concerning the basis of these accounts in Wittgenstein apart, it is difficult to construe such sentences as 'God is good (God is infinitely good)' and 'God is loving (God is infinitely loving)' as pictures from another standpoint, namely that of traditional Christian belief. On the proposed account the question of such sentences expressing true or false propositions cannot arise, since, as we have seen neither ordered arrangements of pictorial symbols, images, etc., nor functions of these (pictures), can be said to express anything true or false. Yet traditional Christianity has maintained

101

that in some sense such sentences as 'God is loving (God is infinitely loving)' express true propositions or at least express something which is true. On the construction of such sentences as expressing 'grammatical remarks' we can at least give some sense to the notion that they are true, for on such a construction they express necessary truths; on the present construction no such account can in principle be offered. Professor Phillips, anticipating some such objection as that introduced above has written as follows:

> From a consideration of the kind of force which characteristic religious pictures have, we see that to ask whether they are true as if they were would-be empirical propositions is to ask the wrong kind of question. It is of the utmost philosophical importance to recognise that for the believer these pictures constitute truths, truths which form the essence of lifes meaning for them. To ask someone whether he thinks these beliefs are true is not to ask him to produce evidence for them but rather to ask him whether he can live by them, whether he can digest them, whether they constitute food for him.[21]

This account is not adequate to meet the demands of traditional Christian belief. Whilst Phillips is correct in maintaining that the religious 'remarks' which he construes as 'pictures' are not would-be empirical propositions in the sense that empirical evidence can be adduced in support of them, empirical propositions are not the only kind of propositions which can be true or false, and not all evidence is empirical evidence. In terms of traditional Christian belief such 'remarks' are held to express true propositions and the evidence for them is the authority of Christ himself. Phillips simply cannot cater for this consideration in his account. Further, if for the tenets of Christianity to be true is for people to be able to live by certain 'pictures', finding that such 'pictures' give sustenance to them, then:

(a) No account of Divine revelation can be offered since there can be no source of such revelation and further, even if Phillips can give an account of what it would be to say (on his account) that these 'pictures' constitute a revelation, it is difficult to see what account he could give other than in terms

102

of their pragmatic force, which makes a nonsense of the notion of revelation as traditionally conceived.

(b) No account can be offered of Divine Grace, since *ex hypothesi* there can be no source of such grace and on this account the whole onus is on whether a man can or cannot, of his own volition, live by these 'pictures'.

(c) It is quite implausible to say that for Christianity to be true *is* for it, as a system of 'pictures', to be pallatable to certain intellectual appetites or for certain people to be able to live by it. How does Phillips cope with (i) the existence of Martyrs, and (ii) the possibility of heretics on this view? On such a view a martyr would simply be someone who had died since he could not reject a certain 'picture' or could not accept an alternative 'picture'; I have yet to hear of anyone who is prepared to give their life for the sake of a 'picture' or because he cannot tolerate another 'picture'. I cannot even conjecture what Phillips would say about heretics; they must in some way or other get certain pictures *wrong*, they cannot be said to have a *different* set of 'pictures' or at least it is not clear how they can and even if they *can* be so said they are in no worse a position than those who have the 'true' or 'correct' set (but we cannot speak of 'true' or 'correct' here).

(d) On this account of 'truth' to say Christianity is true is to say that Christianity is true *for me* (who accepts it) or is not true *for you* (who does not accept it). This renders the notion of truth quite vacuous in this context, for it is tantamount to saying 'I find Christianity pallatable and I am able to live by it'.

I find these objections and difficulties sufficient to conclude that Professor Phillips has not offered a satisfactory answer to the problem of how the 'picture' view of sentences in Christian discourse can cope with the problem of truth in Christianity; the attempted answer only succeeds in making the concept of truth in Christianity a vacuity. It may be replied that it is a mis-reading of Phillips' position to think that at least part of his aim is to offer an account of Christian belief which would concur with an accepted tradition; he is, after all, it might be said, offering a *possible* account, not an account which the Church has accepted or a tradition which the Church has accepted. The serious problem is whether this account *is* a possible account on the grounds that it radically distorts the tradition; this question, however, is the proper subject of a larger and fuller inquiry.

I venture to suggest that the reason why some people have adopted the view that we should regard sentences containing the word 'God' as pictures and having the possible roles of a picture is that they have started from a certain kind of example, namely that kind of example in which a picture (in the sense of a myth) or a metaphor is central – for example, God's creation of the world as set forth in either Genesis 1 or the first part of Genesis 2 or 'God's eye sees everything'. It can be maintained that even the orthodox would regard the Genesis account of the creation of the world as a picture in the sense of a myth.[22] But such a picture is introduced into the language of religious belief in contrast with some part of that language which is *not* mythical or pictorial and at least part of that non-mythical, non-pictorial part is constituted by instances of sentences of the very form I have been concerned with, viz. 'God is good' ('God is infinitely good'); 'God is loving' ('God is infinitely loving'). Again, no one would want to deny that 'God's eye sees everything' presents us with a kind of picture, for the idea of God's eye is indeed a metaphor, but from such a consideration it does not follow that every sentence concerning God can be so regarded; not every sentence concerning God has a metaphorical use. Indeed in order for the metaphorical remarks occurring in religious belief to be correctly understood, there must be some non-metaphorical remarks within theology and religious belief to which such metaphors can be related. Again, if we cannot locate *some* non-mythical, non-pictorial remarks in theology and religious belief, the condition of such myths and 'pictures' having a sense is withdrawn. Not *all* theological language or religious language can be regarded as myth, metaphor, or as presenting a picture; otherwise the idea of a myth, metaphor or picture *within* theology or religious discourse would cease to have sense.

3. At this point it might be commented that sentences of the form I am considering have many different functions in religious discourse. For example, such sentences may form part of petitionary prayers in which God is addressed as infinitely merciful, good, loving, wise, etc., form parts of prayers of thanksgiving or of hymns or psalms of praise and thanksgiving;

104

form parts of homilies, sermons, exhortations and parts of the various rites of the Church. It is not to be denied that such sentences can and do perform such roles and in performing such roles they cannot be regarded as expressing anything which is either true or false; in short a performative function is not to be confused with a descriptive function. The suggestion however that *all* uses of such sentences can be specified in terms of their functions as parts of prayers, petitions, thanksgivings, etc., i.e. that *all* uses of such sentences are liturgical cannot be entertained on the grounds that (a) the role of such sentences to address God as merciful, loving, etc. presupposes for its legitimate sense that God is of such a nature; the addressing of God in such a style is not a mere formality; (b) the use of such sentences to petition God supposes that God is of such a nature that the petition might be granted; (c) the use of such sentences to thank God supposes that God is of such a nature to do and has done that which is worthy of thanks; (d) the use of such sentences in homilies, exhortations, sermons, etc., supposes that God has a certain nature and wills and commands certain things: (e) the use of such sentences in the various rites of the Church is only intelligible against the background of God being of a certain nature and having done and commanded certain things to be done. If we deny that such liturgical uses of such sentences work against the background of a non-liturgical, i.e. propositional use and depend for their intelligibility upon some non-liturgical use, then we are forced to say that all there is to religious belief is the practice of certain rites and ceremonies plus exhortations to live a certain kind of life. In this case such religious practices are quite irrational and we shall have to explain the rites and ceremonies of the Church in terms of the satisfaction of some psychological need, as indeed some have been tempted so to do.[23] Such an account however would be inadequate since it takes no cognisance of the agents reasons for either performing such rites or ceremonies or participating in such rites or ceremonies; indeed such an account would necessarily reject any reference to reasons at all.

Such a propositional use of sentences of the form I have been considering, is, I contend, to be found in the 'formal' statements of the Church, for example, in the Thirty Nine Articles of the Church of England, in the Westminster Confessional, and in that part of the *Summa Theologica* (Ia, q6) which discusses the

105

goodness of God. If it be said that such 'formal' statements, in at least the first two cases mentioned, are not to be regarded as a propositional use of such sentences since they are 'articles of Faith' or 'confessions', it must be replied that whilst being articles of Faith expresses a function of such sentences (and likewise being a confession expresses a function of such sentences), the possibility of such sentences having such functions (having such a 'performative' role), *presupposes* that such sentences have the function of expressing true propositions, for the question of *what is ascribed to or affirmed* can always be raised concerning any article of Faith and the question of *what is confessed* concerning any confession. In relation to the third case, i.e. that from the *Summa Theologica*, it is clear that no such account in terms of the function of ascribing, affirming, or confessing can be given. Aquinas would hold that such sentences in such a context express eternally true propositions, for in such a context, i.e. that of Natural Theology, they form part of a science in Aristotle's sense.[24]

5 Some Attempted Conclusions

In the light of my discussion in the last chapter I conclude that:

(1) Sentences of the form I have been considering cannot be regarded as either (a) expressing pictures or (b) being pictures or (c) presenting pictures which play a certain role in the life of the believer, and that attempts to develop a 'picture' theory of such sentences, in addition to being based initially on false assumptions present in certain cited writings of the later Wittgenstein, are either internally inconsistent, lacking in decision procedure and open to crucial objections from the standpoint of traditional belief (in the case of Professor Phillip's account) *or* are open to the charge of introducing a vacuous notion of 'logical connection' on the basis of an unintelligible use of the notion of 'entailment' and to a charge of incompleteness (in the case of Dr Hudson's account); and

(2) that such sentences cannot, without, at the very least, disastrous consequences, be regarded as remarks of 'grammar' in Wittgenstein's sense.

In the light of the inadequacies of the above discussed accounts and the necessity of having at least *some* propositional uses of sentences of the form: 'God is F 'in order that (a) we can introduce parables and parabolic discourse into the discourse of Christianity (or account for the introduction of such discourse already present); (b) we can introduce myth and metaphor (or sensibly account for its introduction) into such discourse; (c) we can introduce the language of rites and ceremonies (or rationally account for its introduction), it is necessary to turn again to the question of the logical form of the propositions putatively expressed by such sentences. However, I have earlier argued that in the light of the conflicting status of the term 'God', not only can no single account be offered but that if we are to meet the requirement that the same term is introduced by "God" on different occasions of use, i.e. in differing contexts, then no account can be offered. In the light of this situation the most one could hope to do would be to *construct* a scheme in which 'God' has a single status and in terms of which a consistent account of the form of proposition expressed by sentences of the form 'God is F' could be offered. In the light of the difficulties I have raised for the contention that 'God' is a proper name and the special difficulties concerning abstract terms, it might be pressed that the only scheme which could be so offered would be one in whch:

(1) 'God' is introduced as a descriptive predicable term for all uses of "God";
(2) sentences of the form 'God is F' express propositions of the form '∃x (Gx . Fx)' where 'x' can take as values the names of eternal, a-spatio-temporal individuals;[1]
(3) we could specify in theory what would constitute whatever is such that it is God failing to be F, even though this state of affairs could never come to be since propositions expressed by sentences of the form 'God is F', *if true*, are true for all times, i.e. *if true*, then always have been true and always will be true. In this sense such propositions are necessarily true, are necessary propositions in that sense recently expounded by Dr Kenny and, it seems, present in Aquinas.[2]

But for such a scheme to be a starter a case would have to be advanced for maintaining that there can be eternal, a-spatio-temporal individuals which do not depend for their identity or individuation upon temporal, spatial, or spatio-temporal individuals of certain kinds or sorts and I have advanced considerations against such a case being made out. Even if these considerations are not, as I have contended, fatal, such that the above scheme is a starter, such a scheme would, even so, only be a *construction*. To introduce 'God' as a descriptive predicable term for all uses of "God" would necessarily omit central features of the occurrences of 'God' in Christian language, for example, those features that require that 'God' be an abstract term or those features which might lead one to suggest that 'God' is a 'Formal Concept' as opposed to a 'Proper Concept' (in Wittgenstein's sense of these terms, cf. *Tractatus*, op. cit.), viz. such features as 'God' not being able to be precursed by a number or by 'the same' or being able to replace the blank in the formula '—— exists', which such features were amongst those pressed against the consideration that 'God' is a descrip-

108

tive predicable term in the early part of Chapter Three.[3] Again, such a scheme could not cater for important aspects of Christian belief about God, for example, doctrines to the effect that God is the principle of all being or, if my objections to Geach hold and my account of Aquinas is correct, the doctrine that God is his essence or nature. Further, the Protestant doctrine that 'God does not exist; He is eternal' would have to be re-written as a doctrine to the effect that God does exist in that some, i.e. at the least one, a-spatio-temporal, i.e. eternal, individual satisfies that description and it is, to say the least, a matter of doubt whether any Protestant theology which has its roots in Kierkegaard could permit such a re-writing as an expression of that doctrine.

It might now be said that such difficulties arise and have arisen throughout the course of this book precisely because I have considered too wide a range of occurrences of the term 'God'; in that I have taken points from Catholic, Anglican and Protestant theologies and beliefs I have worked on the initial assumption that Christian belief forms a homogeneous whole, whereas, it might be suggested, Catholics and 'extreme' Protestants (e.g.) do not simply hold different positions within one and the same tradition, even though those positions represent the limits of the Christian spectrum, but have different traditions, i.e. worship different entities. A case for such a suggestion might be[5] made by pointing out that whilst Catholicism holds that it is both possible and necessary to prove, i.e. demonstrate, the existence of God from non-theistic premises, Protestant Theology, in at least that form which has its roots or its ultimate expression in Kierkegaard, holds that it is not in principle possible to prove the existence of God from non-theistic premises and hence necessarily not necessary. Indeed it is held to be a fundamental misunderstanding of the Christian God to attempt such a proof. But even if we were to allow such a suggestion to stand, and it is not to be lightly dismissed even in these days of ecumenism, not even Catholic Theology can allow that 'God' is simply a descriptive predicable term – at least not in so far as it follows Aquinas in maintaining that God is a self-subsisting Form and my account of Aquinas is correct, and in so far as it maintains that God is the principle of all being.

Again, even if a case could be made out for the possibility of

109

necessarily non-spatio-temporal individuals, such that it might be possible to demonstrate that there is at the least one and at the most one such individual and that such an individual was introduced as the bearer of the proper name 'God' and we were to construct a scheme in which 'God' solely had this use such that we could construe some sentences of the form 'God is F' as expressing propositions of a subject predicate kind, such a scheme would only be a *construction* and could not cater for (a) those considerations put forward in Chapter One which led me to reject the thesis that 'God' is a proper name; (b) those considerations which might lead us to suggest that 'God' is a 'Formal Concept'; (c) those considerations which led me to maintain the thesis that in some contexts 'God' is an abstract term.

Again, even if it could be shown that there are no inherent difficulties in the notion of an abstract term *per se* or that the arguments I have advanced against abstract terms *per se* in the latter part of Chapter Three are ultimately spurious, such that 'God' could be introduced as such a term and that an account of the form of proposition expressed by sentences of the form 'God is F' (where 'God' is such an abstract term) be offered, such an introduction could not cater for some features which the term 'God' actually exhibits – for example, that it can be precursed by a number or by 'the same' or replace the blank in the formula '―― exists'.

I am thus led to the conclusion that there are fatal difficulties for any scheme in which 'God' is introduced as having a single status such that we can offer a coherent and consistent account of the form of proposition expressed by sentences of the form 'God is F'. No such scheme can cope with the manifold and inconsistent logic of 'God'. It is my earnest hope that as a result of my present inquiry in this essay further light can be shed on the problems and difficulties which I have raised, which problems and difficulties must be the source of perpetual concern both for those who have an earnest desire to believe but are unsure what is involved in Christian belief since in any attempt to determine the logical status of 'God' one meets with a mare's nest of difficulties and confusions, and for those, who like the writer of this present essay, struggle on in the context of the Church.

110

Notes and References

Chapter 1

1. *Book of Common Prayer:* (i) Second Collect at Evening Prayer; (ii) Collect in the Litany; (iii) Prayer for those to be admitted to Holy Orders.

2. *Book of Common Prayer:* (iv) A prayer for the Royal Family at Evening Prayer; (v) a prayer for the Clergy and People at Evening Prayer; (vi) Collect for Trinity XIII.

3. Cf. P. T. Geach, 'Good and Evil', *Analysis*, vol. 17 (1956) pp. 34–42.

4. *Book of Common Prayer:* (vii) Collect for Trinity V; (viii) Collect for Trinity VII; (ix) Collect for Trinity IX.

5. G. E. M. Anscombe and P. T. Geach, *Three Philosophers* (Basil Blackwell, Oxford, 1961) p. 8.

6. P. T. Geach, *Reference and Generality* (Cornell University Press, New York, 1962) p. 39.

7. Ibid.

8. G. E. M. Anscombe, *An Introduction to Wittgenstein's Tractatus.* (Hutchinson University Library, London, 1959) p. 41.

9. Geach, *Reference and Generality*, pp. 31–2.

10. Miss Ishiguro in 'Use and Reference of Names' in Peter Winch (ed.) *Studies in the Philosophy of Wittgenstein* (Routledge and Kegan Paul, London, 1969) has argued against this, but to accept her case would commit one to the view that one could not determine what any given name stood for without knowing the truth conditions of all the propositions in which that name occurs. (See also Geach, *Reference and Generality*, pp. 25–6.)

11. See 'On Denoting' reprinted in R. C. Marsh (ed.), *Bertrand Russell – Logic and Knowledge* (George Allen & Unwin, London, 1956).

12. It is, I contend, only by a radical conflation of names and predicables that Quine so construes proper names and produces the artificial predicate 'socratises'.

111

13. In Basil Mitchell (ed.), *Faith and Logic* (George Allen & Unwin, London, 1957) pp. 9–30.

14. Ibid., p. 85.

15. Ibid.

16. Ibid., p. 10.

17. Ibid., p. 30.

18. Cf. also H. H. Farmer, *Towards Belief in God* (S.C.M., Press, London 1942).

19. Cf. H. H. Farmer, *Revelation and Religion* (James Nisbet & Co., Welwyn, 1954); Martin Bubert, *I and Thou* (T. & T. Clark, Edinburgh, 1937); Emil Brunner *The Divine – Human Encounter* (S.C.M. Press, London, 1944).

20. In Mitchell (ed.), *Faith and Logic*, pp. 31–83 (cf. especially pp. 39–40).

21. Cf. Geach, *Reference and Generality*, p. 39.

22. We must distinguish carefully between 'One' as the proper name of a number and 'one' which forms an essential part of a predicate, i.e. which belongs to a concept in Frege's sense (cf. Gottlob Frege, *The Foundations of Arithmetic*, trans. J. L. Austin (Basil Blackwell, Oxford, 1950) p. 66.

23. *Summa Theologica* Ia, q3, a5.

24. Mitchell (ed.), *Faith and Logic*, p. 57.

25. Ibid., pp. 59–60.

26. *De Trinitate*, VII, 4, 7.

27. Cf. M. Durrant, *Theology and Intelligibility*, Chapter 5. (To be published in D. Z. Phillips (ed.), 'Studies in Ethics and the Philosophy of Religion', Routledge & Kegan Paul, London.)

28. Cf. Chapter 3.

29. Cf. Wittgenstein's *Tractatus*, 4.1272.

30. L. Wittgenstein, *Philosophical Investigations*, trans. G. E. M. Anscombe (Blackwell, Oxford, 1953).

31. Cf. Norman Malcolm, 'Anselm's Ontological Arguments', reprinted in D. Z. Phillips (ed.), *Religion and Understanding* (Basil Blackwell, Oxford, 1967) p. 47.

32. Cf. *Religious Studies*, vol. 4 pp. 229–43.

33. In *Logic and Knowledge*, pp. 232–3.

34. Geach, *Reference and Generality*.

35. See his essay on Aquinas in Anscombe and Geach, *Three Philosophers*.

36. Cf. Chapter 3.

37. Anscombe and Geach, *Three Philosophers*, p. 109.

38. Cf. G. Frege, *Foundations of Arithmetic*, p. 59; also 'On Concept and Object' in P. Geach and M. Black, *Philosophical Writings of Gottlob Frege* (Basil Blackwell, Oxford 1952) pp. 42–55.

39. Ibid

40. Cf. *Sophia*, vol x, no. 1, April 1971.

41. I think this reformulation evades Attfield's objection (op. cit.).

42. Cf. Frege, 'On Concept and Object' (op. cit.).

43. Attfield and others might argue that proper names do not have meanings, that there is no 'nominal essence' of proper names. I contend that this view is quite implausible and concur with Geach's argument (cf. Geach, *Reference and Generality*, Chapter 2, pp. 43–4).

44. R. Rhees, *Without Answers* (Routledge & Kegan Paul, London, 1969) pp. 128–9.

45. Cf. Aquinas, *Summa Theologica*, Ia, q52, a1.

46. J. Blakey, *Intermediate Pure Mathematics* (Cleaver-Hume Press, London, 1953) p. 1.

47. Frege, *Foundations of Arithmetic*, p. 90.

48. Cf. Plato, *Parmenides* 137Cff. (cf. also note 22 above).

49. In Frege's sense.

50. Cf. Frege, *Foundations of Arithmetic*, p. 60; also 'On Concept and Object' (op. cit.).

51. Ibid., Reply to objection 2.

52. Aristotle, *Posterior Analytics* A, Chs. 4, 6.

Chapter 2

1. Cf. Chapter 3, pp. 55–6

2. P. F. Strawson, *Individuals* (Methuen & Co. Ltd, London, 1959) p. 16.

3. Ibid.

4. Geach, *Reference and Generality*, pp. 38–9.

5. Reprinted in Anthony Flew (ed.), *Essays in Conceptual Analysis* (Macmillan & Co., London, 1963) p. 30.

6. That all attempts to explicate meaning in terms of use are doomed to failure see 'The Irreducibility of Meaning' by Robin Attfield and myself forthcoming in *Nous*.

113

7. Cf. P. F. Strawson, 'Singular Terms and Predication' reprinted in his collection *Logico–Linguistic Papers* (Methuen & Co. Ltd, London, 1971) p. 59.

8. Ibid.

9. My parentheses.

10. Ibid., pp. 59–60.

11. Cf. Chapter 1.

12. Strawson, *Logico–Linguistic Papers*, p. 63.

13. There are indeed such difficulties but to discuss them is technically outside the range of this essay.

14. Geach, *Reference and Generality*, pp. 38–46.

15. Ibid., p. 43.

16. Ibid., p. 45.

17. Frege, *Foundations of Arithmetic*, p. 60; 'On Concept and Object' (op. cit.), p. 47.

18. 'On Concept and Object', p. 47.

19. Ibid.

Chapter 3

1. *Summa Theologica*, Ia, q3, a2.

2. Reprinted in Peter Geach, *God and the Soul* (Routledge & Kegan Paul, London, 1969) pp. 42–64.

3. Cf. M. Durrant, *Theology and Intelligibility*, Chapter 2, Appendix B.

4. Cf. Malcolm, 'Anselm's Ontological Arguments' in *Religion and Understanding*, op. cit.

5. Dr Kenny, *The Five Ways* (Routledge & Kegan Paul, London, 1969), p. 56.

6. Geach, *God and the Soul*, p. 57.

7. For a fuller discussion of some of the difficulties I think are involved in Geach's position see M. Durrant, 'Professor Geach and the Gods of the Heathen', *Religious Studies*, vol. 7, no. 3, pp. 227–31.

8. For some further argument against the thesis that 'God' is a descriptive predicable in the sense of either a 'matter' term or a 'count' term see Durrant, *Theology and Intelligibility*, Chapter 2.

9. Cf. Chapter 1 above and pp. 49–51 below.

10. Cf. Durrant, *Theology and Intelligibility*, Chapter 5.

11. For an interesting discussion of Quine's position see Fred Sommers 'Predicability', Max Black (ed.), *Philosophy in America* (Muirhead Library of Philosophy, George Allen and Unwin, London, 1965) pp. 262–81.

12. Geach, *God and the Soul*, pp. 42–64.

13. Aristotle, *Metaphysics*, ibid.

14. G. E. L. Owen, 'Aristotle on the Snares of Ontology', R. Bambrough (ed.), *New Essays on Plato and Aristotle* (Routledge & Kegan Paul, London, 1965) p. 78.

15. Geach, *God and the Soul*, pp. 17–29. Cf. also 'What do we think with?' in the same book.

16. Aristotle, *De Anima*, II, 1.

17. Geach, *God and the Soul*, pp. 57, 109; Anscombe and Geach, *Three Philosophers*, p. 109.

18. Anscombe and Geach, *Three Philosophers*, p. 89.

19. For some objections to the analogy and to Geach's interpretation see Kenny, *The Five Ways*, pp. 83ff.

20. Quine's programme for the elimination of names is open to just this objection.

21. Anscombe and Geach, *Three Philosophers*, p. 79.

22. Ibid., pp. 77–8.

23. Ibid., p. 80.

24. Plato would have offered just such an account.

25. *Summa Theologica* Ia, q3, a2 reply to objection 3.

26. Plato, *Parmenides*, 133 D.

27. Cf. Flew and MacIntyre (eds.), *New Essays in Philosophical Theology* (S.C.M. Press, London, 1955), pp. 4–5.

28. Cf. 'Form and Existence', *Proceedings of the Aristotelian Society*, New Series, vol. LV, 1954–5, p. 260.

29. Cf. my earlier argument in Chapter 1.

30. Cf. 'Form and Existence' as reprinted in *God and the Soul*, p. 58.

31. Such terms meet with those requirements which Frege sets out for a term to be a unit of counting in its own right (cf. *Foundations of Arithmetic*, pp. 59–66; 'On Concept and Object', op. cit.; cf. also Durrant, *Theology and Intelligibility*, Chapter 5).

32. Aristotle, *Metaphysics* 1028 a 12; 1016 b 16.

33. Ibid., 996 b 8; 1013 a 27ff; 1017 b 22ff, 1043 a 17ff.

34. Anscombe and Geach, *Three Philosophers*, p. 49.

35. Aristotle, *Metaphysics*, 1022 a 15; 1043 a 33–5.

36. Strawson, *Individuals*, p. 227.

37. Cf. Geach, *God and the Soul*, pp. 46ff; Anscombe and Geach, *Three Philosophers*, p. 78.

38. Cf. Plato, *Parmenides*. This is Parmenides' point that the Forms cannot exist in separation from particulars.

39. Geach, *God and the Soul*, pp. 46–7.

40. Flew and MacIntyre (eds.), *New Essays in Philosophical Theology*, pp. 4–5.

41. Aristotle, *Nicomachean Ethics* 1142 b 2ff.

Chapter 4

1. D. Z. Phillips (ed.), *Religion and Understanding*, p. 66; cf. also D. Z. Phillips, *The Concept of Prayer* (Routledge & Kegan Paul, London, 1965) p. 8.

2. *Summa Theologica* Ia, q3, a1.

3. One might raise the question 'How does this construction cope with God's action concerning those who sin against the Holy Spirit?'

4. L. Wittgenstein, *Lectures and Conversations on Aesthetics, Psychology and Religious Belief*, ed. Cyril Barrett (Basil Blackwell, Oxford, 1966).

5. Ibid., p. 59.

6. My parentheses.

7. D. Z. Phillips, *Death and Immortality*, in New Studies in the Philosophy of Religion, edited by W. D. Hudson (Macmillan, 1970) pp. 64–5.

8. E. Daitz, 'The Picture Theory of Meaning' reprinted in *Essays in Conceptual Analysis*, pp. 53–74.

9. Ibid., pp. 60ff.

10. Phillips, *Death and Immortality*, chapter 4.

11. Ibid., pp. 65–6.

12. Ibid., p. 66.

13. Ibid., pp. 64ff.

14. Cf. Durrant 'God and Analogy', *Sophia*, vol. VIII, no. 3, pp. 11–24.

15. *St Luke*, Chapter 15.

16. My parentheses.

17. Phillips, *Death and Immortality*, p. 66.

18. In *Talk of God* (Royal Institute of Philosophy Lectures, 1967–8) vol. 2 (Macmillan) pp. 36–51.

19. My italics.

20. For some further discussion of Hudson's position see M. Durrant, 'The use of "Pictures" in Religious Belief', *Sophia*, vol. x, no. 2, pp. 16–21.

21. Phillips, *Death and Immortality*, p. 71.

22. Flew and Mackinnon, 'Creation' in *New Essays in Philosophical Theology*, pp. 170–186.

23. I have in mind here the attempts of 'Functional Analysts' to give an account of religious belief and practices.

24. Aristotle, *Posterior Analytics* A, 4, 6.

Chapter 5

1. It might be contended that it is implausible to suggest that sentences of the form 'God is F' express propositions of the form '∃x(Gx . Fx)'; rather, in order to cater for the Christian assertion that there is only one God, such sentences should be construed as expressing propositions of the form '∃x(Gx . for all y, Gy only if y =x . Fx), where 'x' and 'y' can take as values the names of eternal, a-spatio-temporal individuals. Such a construction, however, would demand that 'God' be not simply a descriptive predicable, but a definite description of the form 'The one and only F'.

2. Dr Kenny, 'God and Necessity', Williams and Montefiore (eds.), *British Analytical Philosophy* (Routledge & Kegan Paul, London, 1966) pp. 131–51; cf. especially pp. 147–8.

3. It cannot be rigorously maintained that 'God' is *solely* a 'Formal Concept' in Wittgenstein's sense, for 'Formal Concepts' cannot occur as propositional items, yet as I have argued at the end of Chapter Four there must be *some* sentences in which 'God' occurs which can be taken as expressing propositions.